PRAISE FOR
GLOBAL
MIND
CHANGE

"Harman makes it possible for anyone interested in the progress of the human species to journey with him into an arena of human possibilities that, quite literally, is breathtaking."

—**Norman Cousins**

"Superb! A wonderfully concise and profoundly hopeful guide to the great transformation now occurring on our beautiful planet."

—**Hazel Henderson, author of *Creating Alternative Futures***

"Remarkable. . . . It is a book that should be widely read. Willis Harman has spent his life stimulating thoughts, piercing frontiers, and enlarging our comprehensive scope of universal knowledge."

—**Claiborne Pell, United States Senator**

"Willis Harman's *Global Mind Change* . . . gives us hope . . . a sophisticated hope based on psychological understanding of the deeper roots of the human mind. . . . I recommend this book to everyone interested in either inner or outer growth and peace."

—**Charles T. Tart, Ph.D.**
Professor of Psychology, University of California, Davis

"Willis Harman has been a provocative thinker for many years. *Global Mind Change* pulls together his ideas and moves our cultural thinking forward dramatically. We see how our models determine our directions and the ways in which we can create a more desirable world."

—**Robert Theobald, author of *The Rapids of Change***

"Thought provoking and absorbing. . . . It's refreshing to read a title with such an approach, and such an optimistic vision of future change."

—*Midwest Review of Books*

"A remarkable, comprehensive, provocative book that offers some real philosophical insights."

—*Bay City Times*

GLOBAL MIND CHANGE

THE NEW AGE REVOLUTION IN THE WAY WE THINK

WILLIS HARMAN, PH.D.

WARNER BOOKS

A Warner Communications Company

Warner Books Edition

Copyright © 1988 by the Institute of Noetic Sciences

This Warner Books edition is published by arrangement with
the Institute of Noetic Sciences, 475 Gate Five Road, Suite 300,
P.O. Box 97, Sausalito, CA 94966-0097

Warner Books, Inc., 666 Fifth Avenue, New York, NY 10103

W A Warner Communications Company

Printed in the United States of America

First Warner Books Printing: September 1990

10 9 8 7 6 5 4 3 2 1

Library of Congress Cataloging-in-Publication Data

Harman, Willis W.
   Global mind change : the promise of the last years of the
twentieth century / by Willis Harman. — Warner Books ed.
      p.   cm.
   Originally published: 1st ed. : Indianapolis, Ind. : Knowledge
Systems, © 1988.
   Includes bibliographical references (p.
   ISBN 0-446-39147-6
   1. Social change.   2. Attitude change.   I. Title.
[HM101.H28   1990]
303.4—dc20   89-21492
                                                              CIP

Cover design by Harold Nolan

About the Book

*Perhaps the only limits to the human mind
are those we believe in.*

If the world that science tells us about is *reality*, how does it happen that we don't feel more at home in it?

The factors and forces to bring about a *global mind change* are already set in motion.

Throughout history, the really fundamental changes in societies have come about not from dictates of governments and the results of battles but through vast numbers of people changing their minds—sometimes only a little bit.

Some of these changes have amounted to profound transformations—for instance the transition from the Roman empire to medieval Europe, or from the Middle Ages to modern times. Others have been more specific, such as the constitution of democratic governments in England and America, or the termination of slavery as an accepted institution. In the latter cases, it is largely a matter of people recalling that no matter how powerful the economic or political or even military institution it persists because it has legitimacy, and that legitimacy comes from the perceptions of people. People give legitimacy and they can take it away. A challenge to legitimacy is probably the most powerful force for change to be found in history.

To the empowering principle that the people can withhold legitimacy, and thus change the world, we now add another. By deliberately changing the internal image of reality, people can change the world.

The Henry Rolfs Book Series
of the
Institute of Noetic Sciences

The Noetic Sciences Book Series is dedicated to Henry Rolfs, a long-standing member of the Board of Directors, whose leadership, generosity, and personal courage have been instrumental in establishing the Institute of Noetic Sciences.

Dedication

I wish to dedicate this book to four
persons who have profoundly affected
the latter part of my life:
Alfred M. Hubbard and Judith Skutch Whitson,
who were my teachers in the truest sense, and
Paul N. Temple and Henry Rolfs, whose generosity,
through the Institute of Noetic Sciences, has given
me the freedom to serve in the best way I know.

Acknowledgments

I would like to acknowledge with gratitude
the insights that have come to me from many people,
particularly Brendan O'Regan, Tom Hurley and
Barbara McNeill, staff members at the
Institute of Noetic Sciences.
Thanks also to Institute editor Carol Guion
and layout artist Leona Jamison
for their invaluable aid in producing the book,
and to Art Holman for his painting on the cover
and chapter heads.

Contents

Foreword

The first twenty years of my professional life were spent teaching electrical engineering and systems analysis at a major university. The next twenty were as a social scientist and futurist in a contract research organization, helping clients in government and business do strategic planning over a very wide range of practical policy issues. My particular task was to help them think about the issues in the context of the future environment in which the consequences of their decisions would manifest. To deal with these puzzles full time, day after day, was an unusual privilege, and I learned much. As the years went on, I found that a picture was forming in my mind of the meaning of our times and of many plausible alternative futures. The picture got clearer, and by the time I retired from that career and moved on to a third (the present one), I had little remaining doubt about the fundamental nature of the transformation we are living through. Although I was aware that some aspects seemed preposterous to most, I was convinced (and my conviction continues to strengthen) that the real action today is *changing fundamental assumptions.*

In 1977 I accepted the invitation of Edgar Mitchell and the Board of the Institute of Noetic Sciences to join them in "expanding knowledge of the nature and potentials of the mind, and applying that knowledge to the advancement of health and well-being for humankind and the planet." (The word "noetic", from the Greek word "nous" meaning mind, intelligence, understanding, implies the three ways in which we gain knowledge: the reasoning processes of the intellect, the perception of our experiences through the senses, and the intuitive, spiritual or inner ways of knowing. Noetic Sciences is the systematic study of these all-inclusive ways of knowing, which form the basis for how we see ourselves, each other, and the world.)

Since the work of the Institute is at the heart of the contemporary "paradigm change"—it is precisely in this area that the basic assumptions underlying modern Western society are most called into question—I knew I had found an ideal place to be.

But the task is not easy. People are threatened by the awareness (conscious or unconscious) of impending change in their lives. The prospect that "truths" they have known all their lives might be superseded by some other beliefs can be especially threatening. Thus there is a tendency to "fight back"—to actively oppose the change. Note the fundamentalist reaction in all parts of the globe to modern society's embodiment of change as a way of life—technological change, increasing power of institutions, weakening of older value commitments.

You can imagine that critical examination of the basic assumptions undergirding modern society itself will be all the more threatening. Sociological and historical researches show that during similar revolutionary changes there are, typically, increases in frequency of mental illness, social disruption and use of police to quell the disruption, violent crime, terrorism, religious cultism, and acceptance of sexual hedonism. These signs are, of course, visible today, and they may well intensify before they return to more normal levels. They are all basically responses to the underlying anxiety and uncertainty to the unconscious threat of change.

Understanding the necessity of change probably reduces the threat as one sees that world society can not continue much longer on its current, increasingly nonviable tract. But societal change implies individual change, and it is that which brings on the sharpest anxiety.

The next decade or two are particularly critical. I believe the key challenge is not to try to resist a change that may well be inevitable, nor is it to be zealous in fomenting a change prematurely. It is, rather, trying to help our society understand the nature and necessity of the forces of historical change we are experiencing, to go through the change with mutual cooperation and caring, with as little misery as possible.

Through truth-telling and dialogue and sincere attempts to see the world through the other person's eyes, together we can come to an understanding of what it is that needs doing, and to a joint commitment that it gets done. All my life I have heard the admonition, "Don't just talk; get out there and do something!" The problem is that in times like these we are all too likely to do what turns out to be the wrong thing. If it is to represent the best advice for such uncertain times, the maxim should probably be turned around: *Don't just do something; get out there and talk.*

In this third career what I feel most keenly to be my own mission is to promote that dialogue and contribute to that understanding. This book is a step in that direction; I hope it is a helpful one.

Willis W. Harman
Sausalito, California
September 1987

Introduction

Imagine yourself a historian looking back from some time in the next century. What do you judge the most important thing that happened for the world in the twentieth century? Was it putting a man on the Moon? Or creation of the United Nations? Or the development of nuclear weapons, or of computers and artificial intelligence?

My guess is that it will be something much less conspicuous to those of us who are living now, something whose significance will not be fully apparent for decades to come. It will be something as quiet as a change of mind, a change of mind that is bubbling up out of the unconscious depths, spreading around the world, changing everything.

It is much easier, of course, to answer that question about the seventeenth century. In retrospect, we can easily see that the most important development for the world was not the Thirty Years' War and the Peace of Westphalia, nor the ending of the Ming dynasty in China, nor even the establishment of colonies along the Atlantic seaboard of North America. Most people would probably agree, after some thought, that the winner is that total change of view which we call the scientific revolution. The scientific revolution started in Western Europe and ultimately affected the lives of people all over the Earth, in ways so fundamental it is hard to find a comparable transformation anywhere else in history.

It may seem an outrageous hypothesis that in the last third of the twentieth century we should go through another such basic mind change, one at least as profound and far more rapid. Yet that is the thesis of this book.

We are already well into the mind change. It is altering the way we interpret science; it is drastically modifying our concepts of health care; it is revolutionizing our concepts of education; it is causing major changes in the world of business and finance; it is in the process of delegitimating war and causing a total rethinking of the means of achieving national and global security.

Yet its effects are relatively invisible. It does not show up clearly in survey research on values and lifestyles; its incursion into science appears minor indeed; its examples in the corporate world are impressive, but represent a tiny fraction of the whole. The mind change is perhaps most visible in the reperceiving of health care and total fitness, yet even there its broader implications are not widely and openly discussed.

Few today doubt that the world is going through some sort of structural transition. The evidence suggesting this is omnipresent. How major the structural change will be is more disputable. For some the pattern of a fundamental transformation fairly jumps out of the evidence; for others it is a much more problematic conclusion.

Most of us are hesitant to fancy that we might be living through one of the most fundamental shifts in the history of Western civilization. There is a certain reluctance to appear arrogant about our own times: Doesn't every generation think it is living in a unique historical period?

Yet the possibility must be taken seriously.

This small volume explores the hypothesis that a change is taking place at the most fundamental level of the belief structure of Western industrial society. The book is deliberately small, because its purpose is not to make a case with finality but to stimulate a critical dialogue—references are at the end of the book rather than cited throughout as footnotes. We may not be able to reach consensus on the correct interpretation of our times. But the stakes are high and the attempt is worth making.

However we view it, the present-day world situation is hazardous for civilization. The passengers on planet Earth have a rough passage ahead. Our ability to travel that passage together without a wreck depends on keeping levels of understanding high and anxiety low. Whatever conclusions one reaches participating in this dialogue will increase that needed understanding.

The Alchemist by Rembrandt van Rijn

1

Every transformation . . . has rested on a new metaphysical and ideological base; or rather, upon deeper stirrings and intuitions whose rationalized expression takes the form of a new picture of the cosmos and the nature of man.

— Lewis Mumford

The Scientific Heresy: Transformation of a Society

Once upon a time there was a merchant's son named Nicolaus Copernicus who lived in a small city in Poland. He was a student of law and medicine and mathematics. While still in his twenties he was internationally eminent as a lecturer in mathematics. Most of all, however, he was fascinated by the mathematical intricacies of astronomy. . . .

The story is familiar to everyone. It is retold here because of its contemporary relevance. *Why did the Copernican ideas have such reverberations throughout all of Western Europe? How were such powerful transformational forces set in motion? Suppose a similar transformation were underway today—would we recognize the signs?*

How Christian Europe saw the Universe before Copernicus' time: with the Earth at its center. From a German manuscript, c. 1450.

The Copernican Revolution

Copernicus did not intend a heresy, let alone a "revolution". He was a canon and lawyer at the Cathedral of Frauenberg, the northernmost Catholic diocese in Poland; however he actually devoted much of his time to astronomical studies. As these studies progressed, he became increasingly dissatisfied with the prevailing theoretical system, that of the Alexandrian scholar Ptolemy. This interpretation of the heavens had become firmly entrenched in astronomical thought, virtually as an article of faith, having been used and taught for 14 centuries. It was essentially geocentric, with the firmament a vast spherical crystalline shell revolving around the spherical Earth, and additional mechanisms supporting the Sun, Moon, and planets. The scheme involved an elaborate system of basic circular orbits with superimposed circular motions, called epicycles, added as necessary to account for observed irregularities in the motions of the planets. As observations had become progressively more accurate, more epicycles had to be added, and the whole system had become very unwieldy; it was increasingly difficult to use it for predicting future positions of the heavenly bodies.

The Copernican World System

Nicolaus Copernicus established mathematically *that the Earth moves around the sun in* On the Revolution of the Celestial Spheres (1543).

Copernicus was a competent Greek scholar, and poring over ancient Greek writings he found that some of them had proposed a heliocentric model. In this view the apparent motions of the Sun, Moon, and planets were accounted for by imagining the Earth to rotate daily on its axis, and to revolve around the stationary Sun once a year. At first blush this idea of the Earth moving around the Sun seemed absurd, but when Copernicus applied it to his data (retaining, however, the concept of uniform circular motions) he found the result was æsthetically superior and the model somewhat simpler, when compared with the Ptolemaic system.

At first he only circulated the new ideas quietly among his friends. Meanwhile he developed his argument further with diagrams and mathematical computations. In order to have his model fit astronomical observations he found it necessary to add in numerous complications. In the end, Copernicus' scheme was more elegant than Ptolemy's, but not particularly simpler. (It was Johannes Kepler, a contemporary of Galileo, who later added the notion of elliptical orbits, and formulated the descriptive laws of planetary motion in a far simpler form.)

After three decades of gestation, Copernicus' book *On the Revolution of the Celestial Spheres* was finally published in the year of his death, 1543; a second edition was printed in 1566, and by the end of the century it was well distributed in both Protestant and Catholic countries of Western Europe. His work not only offered an alternative system to the Ptolemaic, on several points it was in direct conflict with the venerated ideas of Aristotle. For instance, Aristotle had argued for the fixity of the Earth, and had taught that bodies fall to the ground because that is their "natural place"—closer to the center of the universe. If Copernicus was right, a new explanation for the behavior of falling bodies was clearly needed, since the Earth no longer held a singular position. (The re-examination of this matter eventually led to Newton's concept of universal gravitation.)

Throughout Western Christendom Aristotle's doctrines had become elevated almost to the level of religious dogma. To some, the new ideas of Copernicus amounted to heresy. To others, however, who had found the Aristotelian dogma stifling of intellectual development, the break with traditional doctrines actually added to the attractiveness of the Copernican theory. (For example, in his *Dialogue on the Two Chief Systems of the World* [1632], Galileo argues pointedly, through discussion between fictional characters, that it is most reasonable that the

Earth moves and is not the center of the universe, and hence Aristotle's whole cosmology is baseless. The feeble defense of Aristotle is left to true-believer Simplicius, whose loyalist arguments are mercilessly attacked.)

The implications of Copernicus' ideas went much farther, however. The dethronement of the Earth from the center of the universe caused profound shock. No longer could the Earth be considered the epitome of creation, for it was only a planet like the other planets. No longer was the Earth the site of all change and decay with the changeless universe encompassing it. And the belief in a correspondence between man, the microcosm, as a mirror of the surrounding universe, the macrocosm, was no longer valid. Actually, the implication was that man might not have such a special place in creation after all. The Copernican ideas became one focus of tremendous controversies in religion, philosophy, and social theory, which set the tenor of the modern mind; they catalyzed a major transition in Western values. In truth, the Copernican revolution amounted to a successful challenge to the entire system of ancient authority, requiring a complete change in the philosophical conception of the universe. It was heresy on the grand scale. Ultimately the "scientific heresy" prevailed, and we now look back on it as an unqualifiedly positive evolutionary step.

Today we know that the transformation in thought which is symbolized by the Copernican episode reached far outside astronomical and philosophical debate; it was part of an even broader transformation, involving the whole way of looking at the world—the transformation that we now call the "scientific revolution". The revolutionaries saw themselves as attacking the traditional ways of thinking and educating. The heresy was directed at the authority system known as Scholasticism. Scholasticism assumed a living world created and guided by God for man's benefit. Its understandings were largely arrived at by citing authorities, either philosophical or scriptural. The primary function of this knowledge was to rationalize sense experience in harmony with revealed religion. In contrast, the new way was empirical: *What is true is what is found by scientific inquiry to be true. Ultimate authority resides in observation and experiment rather than tradition.*

Thus in 1600 an educated man (most educated persons were men) *knew* that the Earth was the center of the cosmos—the seat of change, decay, and Christian redemption—while above it circled the planets and stars, themselves pure and unchanging but moved by some sort of intelligent or divine spirits and also signaling and influencing human events by their locations and aspects. A hundred years later this man's equally Christian descendant, say, his great-grandson, knew (unless he lived in a church-controlled Catholic country) that the Earth was but one of many planets orbiting around one of many stars, moving through and separated by unimaginable distances—all still under the overall guidance of God, but with an important difference. The outlook of the first individual was *teleological*: The universe is alive and imbued with purpose; all creatures are part of a Great Chain of Being, with man between the angels and the lower animals; events are explained by divine purpose or by their function in a meaningful world. To his great-grandson, by contrast, it is essentially a dead universe, constructed and set in motion by the Creator, with subsequent events accounted for by mechanical forces and lawful behaviors. The great-grandfather, as a reasonable man, would accept the overwhelming evidence for the working of enchantments, the occurrence of miracles, the existence of witches and other beings with supernatural powers; his descendant, with equal certainty, would dismiss all those stories as the results of charlatanry and delusion.

The scientific revolution amounted to a new way of seeking and validating knowledge. Knowledge was no longer to be regarded as the established property of a priesthood; it was to be sought in open inquiry, and validated in public by agreed-upon means. Authority was to be sought in experience, rather than orthodoxy. Gradually the role of Providence was transferred to the "natural laws" whereby God was thought to operate. Rather than resulting from the "grace" of Divine intervention, change was increasingly thought of as "evolution" and "stages of advancement" and "material progress". The development of the scientific method (effectively articulated by Francis Bacon) was to bring about creation of vast accumulations of knowledge, and the eventual application of that knowledge to manipulation of the physical environment—to the presumed better-ment of man's condition on Earth. Progress in the arts and sciences became linked with material well-being and spiritual fulfillment—on Earth, rather than at some future time in Heaven.

Nor did the changes stop there. In retrospect, historians and social scientists can now see that the time of Copernicus marked a historic watershed. Before that were centuries of the period we call, broadly, the Middle Ages. After the Copernican impact the course was irrevocably set for what we now call modern times. To be sure, society was changing during the entire period of the Middle Ages. And the changes in one part of Europe were quite different from those in another. And there were other critical developments taking place around the same time as the scientific revolution—the Protestant Reformation, for example, and the economic or capitalist revolution. Furthermore, modern times in the late 1980s are not the same as modern times in the 1950s, or the 1920s. Thus to pick out a particular period as characterized by extraordinary change is somewhat of an artificiality. Still, there is something to that idea of a watershed. Modern times really *are* fundamentally different from the Middle Ages (as those in turn were different from the days of the Roman Empire). The most basic difference is in the underlying view of reality.

Lewis Mumford dealt with this matter of fundamental societal change in a little book published a third of a century ago called *The Transformations of Man* (1956). Some change is taking place all the time, of course, and yet there seem to be particular periods in history when society goes through a more fundamental kind of change, involving all its institutions and even more basic aspects of its culture. Mumford claimed that there have not been more than four or five such "transformations" in the entire history of Western civilization. The most recent one is that marking the end of the Middle Ages.

Mumford observes that "Every transformation of man . . . has rested on a new metaphysical and ideological base; or rather, upon deeper stirrings and intuitions whose rationalized expression takes the form of a new picture of the cosmos and the nature of man." Turning this statement around, the hallmark of transformation is a change at the deepest level of the social structure. Every society ever known rests on some set of largely tacit basic assumptions about *who we are, what kind of universe we are in, and what is ultimately important to us.* Some such set of assumptions can be found to underlie the institutions and mores, patterns of thought and systems of value, that characterize a society. They are typically not formulated or taught because they don't need to be—they are absorbed by each person born into the society as though by osmosis. They are accepted as given, as obviously true—and throughout most of history, by most people, never questioned.

A word made popular by Thomas Kuhn in his study of *The Structure of Scientific Revolutions* (1962) has often been used (sometimes quite loosely) to speak of societal transformation in terms of "paradigm change". When used this way, the dominant paradigm of a society refers to *the basic ways of perceiving, thinking, valuing, and doing, associated with a particular view of reality.* What was so earth-shaking about the Copernican revolution was that *the fundamental view of reality* was shifting; with that shift came major changes in "the basic ways of perceiving, thinking, valuing, and doing"—changes that heralded the modern era.

It would not have been possible for someone in the early part of the seventeenth century, say, to forecast what the consequences of the paradigm change would be—if, indeed, one were able to recognize that such a fundamental belief-system shift was taking place. The best one could have hoped to do would have been to suggest some broad characteristics of the new society. Similarly, if such a transformation is taking place today, we can identify that fact and anticipate some characteristics of post-transformation society. But even that could be extremely useful and is what we will be attempting in this book.

Intimations of Paradigm Change

What manner of evidence could justify such an extravagant comparison as implied by the phrase the *second* Copernican revolution, or might cause us to think of "a *new* heresy" that could change the world as much as the "scientific heresy" did? We shall give a preliminary answer here and then explore the subject in more detail in later chapters.

Roger Sperry of the California Institute of Technology shared the 1981 Nobel Prize in Physiology or Medicine for his work in human split-brain studies. Sperry's research, involving extensive observation of patients whose brains had actually been divided by severing the corpus callosum joining the two halves, showed that there are important differences in functioning between the left and right halves of the brain. (Not as much difference, perhaps, as one might be led to believe from the "left-brain, right-brain" myth of pop psychology, but nevertheless a significant difference.) As an accompaniment to this honor, he was invited to write the lead article for the *1981 Annual Review of Neuroscience*.

Now the traditional summary article in an Annual Review is, as one would gather from the title, a review of the past year's accomplishments in the particular area, plus some strong intimations that much more could be done if there were only more funding. Sperry's paper, entitled "Changing Priorities", did not follow the traditional pattern. Instead, he wrote of the importance of the previously neglected area of subjective experience, and noted a profound development which he describes as follows:

> Current concepts of the mind-brain relation involve a direct break with the long-established materialist and behaviorist doctrine that has dominated neuroscience for many decades. Instead of renouncing or ignoring consciousness, the new interpretation gives full recognition to the primacy of inner conscious awareness as a causal reality.

It is probably not true that Dr. Sperry's colleagues all agree with him, and it is certain that much of the scientific community does not. We shall have to see, later on, what kinds of evidence we can adduce to support this statement. But for the moment just assume it is true. Think of how revolutionary a thought this is, that science should now accommodate consciousness *as a causal reality*.

Throughout most of the history of most kinds of science, scientific research and theory have been based in an implicit metaphysic that is both *reductionistic* and *positivistic*. That is to say, scientists have sought to explain phenomena in terms of more elementary happenings (for example, color explained in terms of wavelength, gas pressure in terms of the motion of the gas molecules); and what is real (or at least discussible) is taken to be that which can be *measured*—that is, what is ultimately discernible to the physical senses, either directly or by the use of scientific instrumentation.

This bias was a most useful one for many purposes. It was especially so for distinguishing scientific explanations from such prescientific interpretations as the whims of the gods, or the intervention of divine grace, or such "natural tendencies" as bodies seeking to come to rest near the center of the universe and nature abhorring a vacuum.

It was the hallmark of the behavioral sciences emphasis of the 1950s that only behavior and forces (stimuli) that were ultimately measurable could be talked about scientifically; the realm of subjective experience could be dealt with only in terms of these externally observable phenomena. Thus the study of consciousness, in scientific terms, was reduced to examination of behavior (such as awareness, responsiveness) that could be observed from outside the organism. Early approaches to dealing with inner conscious awareness in its own terms (that is, introspectionism) had been discredited. Tough-minded behavioral scientists insisted that it would be impossible to build a reliable science based on self-reports of inner, subjective experience (as the phenomenologists and gestaltists had tried to do).

The behavioral predilection became quite strong by mid-century, particularly in the United States. Nevertheless, there remained the sneaking suspicion on the part of many, scientists as well as nonscientists, that something important was being left out. After all, the only experience of reality that we have *directly* is our own conscious awareness. There was something very unnatural about a science which seemed to deny consciousness as a causal reality when everyday experience seemed to confirm again and again that it is my *decision* to act that causes action.

There were other poses that one had to assume in order to be in accord with the sophisticated scientific view of the day, which felt equally artificial. One tried to accept that it is the brain that is real, and conscious awareness is an "epiphenomenon"; the question "Does mind exist?" seemed a serious one. The complex products of creative imagination were supposed to have come about through some sort of random cycling of a brain-computer, together with some kind of selection of "best fit". We were supposed to believe that the complex instinctual behaviors of animals and complex physiological systems such as the two eyes that give us binocular vision had developed through our evolutionary past exclusively as a result of random mutations plus natural selection.

Besides, there were the anomalies to remind us that all was not well with the orthodox scientific worldview. Down through the centuries a variety of anomalous phenomena, including clairvoyant remote viewing, telepathic communication, levitation and teleportation, "instantaneous" spiritual healing, and other "psychic" phenomena, had been reported. Various explanations had been offered as to why these reports were probably mistaken. Famous and competent scientists had arrayed themselves on both sides of the debate. A half-century ago it seemed fairly clear that in spite of the claims of a few persons doing research in parapsychology or "psychic research", the better educated and more sophisticated public felt confident that scientific advance was making the genuineness of the phenomena decreasingly plausible.

What was common to all of these anomalous psychic phenomena was that *mind* seemed to have some effects in the physical world—directly, as in the reported instances of dramatic healing, or indirectly, as in the presumed telepathic communication. But that was true in everyday and commonplace phenomena as well. I decide to raise my right arm, and behold!—it goes up. Attitudes toward one's work bring about tension and stress, and an ulcer results. Patients told that a plain sugar pill has curative powers experience remission of the symptoms of their illness (the placebo effect). In our everyday experience it would seem strained and artificial to deny that what goes on in our minds has effects on our actions. Yet *as scientists*, more than one generation of students were trained to engage in that denial.

It is in the light of these decades of *denial* of consciousness as causal reality that Roger Sperry's pronouncement comes with such impact. It is similar to the impact of Copernicus' theories after centuries of denying that the Earth, being the assumed center of the universe and special focus of Divine attention, could possibly move.

As "the Earth goes around the sun" became the somewhat inadequate summary of the Copernican revolution, so "consciousness as causal reality" is that of the "second Copernican revolution".

But as we recognize "inner conscious awareness as causal reality" we are immediately reminded of Sigmund Freud's insistence that unconscious processes are also causal with regard to our behavior. In assessing how and how much these new elements are going to change things, the most useful starting point for our purposes is the idea of *unconscious beliefs*.

Unconscious Belief

This concept of unconscious beliefs and the extent to which they are capable of shaping and distorting our perceptions of everything around us—and within us—is so central to understanding the global mind change that we shall make a temporary digression to look into it more deeply.

Each of us holds some set of beliefs with which we conceptualize our experience—beliefs about history, beliefs about things, beliefs about the future, about what is to be valued, or about what one ought to do. What may be less obvious is that we have unconscious beliefs as well as conscious ones. (There are many ways in which people have attempted to talk about the processes and contents of the conscious and unconscious minds. In the following discussion we will use a way that is adequately powerful, yet as free as possible of psychological jargon. It employs the concept of the conscious and unconscious *belief system* as introduced by psychologist Milton Rokeach in *The Open and Closed Mind* [1960].)

Persons may not realize they have these unconscious beliefs, but the beliefs can be inferred from behavior—from slips of the tongue, compulsive acts, "body language", and so on. A familiar example from psychotherapy is an unconscious belief in one's inadequacy or inferiority. Individuals may consciously feel adequate and equal, at least most of the time, but under certain circumstances the behavior, body posture, etc. may betray that they unconsciously believe something else to be the case.

Thus we cannot take at face value what a person says he believes. He may be deceiving us deliberately, or he may be rationalizing, not knowing what he deeply believes. We have to infer a person's unconscious beliefs from everything he says and does. That is as true of ourselves as it is of others. We *do not know* what we believe unconsciously, but it is almost certainly not what we consciously believe we believe.

The person's *total belief system* is an organization of beliefs and expectancies that the person accepts as true of the world he or she lives in—verbal and nonverbal, implicit and explicit, conscious and unconscious.

The belief system does not have to be logically consistent; indeed, it probably never is. It may be compartmentalized, containing logically contradictory beliefs which typically do not come into conscious awareness at the same times. The person unconsciously wards off evidence that might reveal such an inner contradiction. Notice that this decision to *not* become consciously aware of something is unconscious. We *choose* as well as believe unconsciously.

The belief system can be conceived of as comprising "concentric" regions or shells. The outermost region contains beliefs that are relatively accessible to conscious awareness and relatively easy to change (as by education). Somewhat more deeply embedded in the system are intermediate-level beliefs, less accessible and more resistant to change. Some of these intermediate-level unconscious beliefs are worked with in psychotherapy (such as the judgments of the "internalized parent"). This intermediate region contains beliefs about the nature of authority (for example, whether I trust my own experience or accept the interpretation of some external authority). In the innermost core of the belief system are basic unconscious assumptions about the nature of the self and its relationship to others, and about the nature of the universe. Typically a person may go through most of life with these core beliefs essentially unchanged. When they do change, the shift is likely to be accompanied by a rather stressful period in the person's life.

Belief systems serve two powerful and conflicting sets of motives at the same time. One is the need for a cognitive framework to interpret new experience—to know and understand and act responsively. The other is the need to ward off threatening aspects of reality. Our belief systems are our way of making sense out of raw experience. However, they may also distort if necessary to preserve the illusion of order—as, for instance, when we "forget" an incident that doesn't "fit in". (Repression of early childhood memories of traumatic experiences is a familiar example.)

A belief system may be defined as *open* to the extent that new data can enter and affect existing beliefs. A person will be open to information insofar as possible, but will unconsciously reject it, screen it out, or alter it insofar as is necessary to ward off threat and anxiety. The closed mind can distort the world and narrow it down to whatever extent is needed to serve these protective goals, and still preserve the illusion of understanding it. The more closed the belief system, the more it can be understood as a tightly woven network of cognitive defenses against anxiety, designed to shield a vulnerable mind.

As was just suggested, we not only believe unconsciously, we also choose unconsciously. This shows up with particular clarity in the case of subliminal perception. In one form of this well-known phenomenon an image is flashed on a screen for a very brief interval—so brief that the person is not consciously aware of having seen anything. However, a physiological response (such as a change in the electrical conductivity of the skin indicating an emotional reaction, or an "event-related potential" in the brain indicating surprise) or a psychological response (for example, influenced free-association) may make it clear that at an unconscious level the person indeed did perceive the image, analyze its meaning, and "choose" an appropriate response.

We need not have gone to the laboratory for an example, of course. Unconscious choosing is evident in everyday life. For instance, I may consciously choose to carry out a certain action which contradicts an unconscious belief (possibly implanted very early in childhood) that the action is *bad*. As a result of an unconscious choice, then, a feeling is telegraphed to the conscious mind—a feeling which we call *guilt*. From still another part of the mind, the deep intuition, may come another choice: to reconcile the conflict and get rid of the guilt feelings.

This is but one example of a more general observation, namely that the typical individual is psychologically fragmented. While the conscious mind is making one set of choices, other fragments of the mind, outside of conscious awareness, are choosing other things. (A rather old-fashioned term describes the individual who had more or less integrated these various fragments into a whole, capable of conflict-free decision: a person of *integrity*.)

Few findings in the social sciences are as well established as the fact that the greater portion of our total mental activity goes on outside of conscious awareness: *We believe, value, choose, and know unconsciously as well as consciously*. Furthermore, our perceptions, values, attitudes, and behavior are influenced far more by what is going on in the unconscious mind than by what is easily accessible to the conscious mind. Although this fact is quite well publicized in our day, we typically live, think, and behave without taking seriously its many implications. (Think, for example, how differently education would be viewed if this fact were taken seriously.)

The way we perceive reality is strongly influenced by unconsciously held beliefs. The phenomena of denial and resistance in psychotherapy illustrate how thoroughly one tends not to see things threatening to deeply held images conflicting with deeply held beliefs. Research on hypnosis, self- and experimenter-expectations, authoritarianism and prejudice, subliminal perception, and selective attention has demonstrated over and over that our perceptions and "reality checks" are influenced, far more than is ordinarily assumed, by beliefs, attitudes, and other mental processes of which a large portion is unconscious. We perceive what we expect, what it has been suggested to us we should perceive, what we "need" to perceive—to an extent that we might be shocked if we realized it consciously.

This influence of beliefs on perception is intensified when a large number of people believe the same thing. Cultural anthropologists have thoroughly documented how persons who grow up in different cultures perceive literally different realities.

The Lesson of Hypnosis

The phenomena of hypnosis, in particular, emphasize dramatically how changes in unconscious beliefs, brought about in this case by suggestion, can alter perception and experience. The suggestion of the hypnotist, for example, can lead the subject to perceive an object or a person that, as far as any onlooker is concerned, really isn't there. Or the subject can be led to fail to perceive something that *is* there. The suggestion of a solid wall can become so real to the subject that his fist is bruised upon "striking" it. The suggestion that a pencil is a hot soldering iron causes it, when laid on the back of the hand, to raise the physical signs of a burn. Acceptance of the hypnotic suggestion that one cannot lift a light object produces a complete inability to do so. On the other hand, a more positive suggestion may lead to the body being able to perform feats it could not otherwise do—form a rigid bridge between two chairs, for example, or lift a heavy weight.

One of the most persuasive yet easily accessible experiences to emphasize this point is the firewalking seminar. Since these seminars were introduced into the United States and Europe in the early 1980s, many thousands of persons have performed this feat, which defies all ordinary expectations about the effect of having flesh come in contact with fire. The essence of the experience is that a smooth bed of burning coals is prepared from a wood fire, and participants, having internalized the suggestion that no harm will ensue, walk barefoot over the coals. The seminars have been carried out with groups ranging in size from a few individuals to several hundred. It is not uncommon for practically everyone to walk, and for practically everyone to be unharmed. Yet the coals are hot (1200 to 1400 degrees Fahrenheit), hot enough to burn the soles of the feet badly in the absence of the protecting belief. Skeptics have claimed that there is a "physical" explanation such as low heat conductivity of charcoal, insulating layer of ash, "leidenfrost effect" of a thin layer of evaporated perspiration. But whatever the intermediating mechanism, the fact remains when people change the unconscious belief that burning coals will barbecue the feet, they are insulated from harm; change the belief back again and severe third-degree burns can result. The experience is powerful because any doubter can experiment by changing the belief and suffering the painful result.

The conclusion we are aiming at does not depend upon any single bit of evidence, so there is no need to strain at explaining away the firewalking phenomenon. (Some skeptics have insisted that it is not necessary to believe that the fire will not harm; it is sufficient to believe strongly that it is not necessary to believe! The suggested "explanations" which appear regularly in the media and scientific literature are much like adding epicycles to the Ptolemaic model—they give comfort to the explainer but add little to our real understanding.) The fundamental fact, powerful and empowering in its implications, is that our experiencing of reality is strongly affected by our internalized beliefs. Our beliefs, in turn, are affected by our experiencing of what we perceive as reality—which most of the time reinforces the beliefs. When it doesn't, we generally feel very uncomfortable—and may be on the way to learning something valuable.

Now each of us, from infancy onward, is subjected to a complex set of suggestions from our social environment, which in effect teaches us how to perceive the world. We may from time to time, especially in early childhood, have experiences that do not conform to this cultural norm—but we eventually "correct" these perceptions and cease experiencing the anomalies, through the power of the socializing process. And so each of us is literally *hypnotized* from infancy to perceive the world the way people in our culture perceive it.

In the modern world this "cultural hypnosis" extends to experiencing a world in which "scientific laws" are always obeyed—whereas in other, more "primitive" cultures, "violations" of these laws may be relatively commonplace. For example, the phenomenon of changing inner beliefs to such an extent that one can with impunity walk barefoot over burning coals, just mentioned, is one which has for centuries been observable in a variety of pre-modern societies. In some cases persons would stand in the fire for half an hour or more, or ladle handfuls of burning coals over their heads in a fiery shower.

In some "primitive" societies remote perception (of the whereabouts of cattle that may have strayed out of sight, or of the well-being of distant relatives for example) is regularly employed. In modern society the phenomenon of "remote viewing" was generally assumed to be physically impossible. How could one possibly "see" what was happening at distances of, perhaps, hundreds or thousands of miles? Yet in recent years, as interest developed in the possible utility of this phenomenon for purposes of military intelligence, there has been research with positive results in both the United States and the Soviet Union.

Reports from the Indian subcontinent of extraordinary capabilities of yogins to mentally control bodily processes were treated with considerable skepticism until the advent of biofeedback training showed that we all have the potential ability, to a far greater extent than had earlier been recognized, to control brain waves, blood flow, heartbeat, and the like.

These several examples emphasize the difficulty of distinguishing the extent to which the "reality" we perceive is peculiar to our cultural hypnosis. We tend to find it curious that other "primitive" or "traditional" cultures should perceive reality in the way they do—so obviously discrepant with the modern scientific worldview. It is harder to entertain the thought that we in modern Western society might have our own cultural peculiarities in the way we perceive the world—that our reality might be as parochial in its way as that of the Middle Ages appears to us now. Since Western science is the "best" knowledge system yet devised, it seems reasonable to consider our values "normal", our predilections "natural", and our perceived and measured world "real".

We now begin to see that comparing our times with the Copernican revolution is not as far-fetched as it may have seemed at first. It was not a comfortable matter, in the early seventeenth century, for an individual to admit into his personal belief system data that challenged the traditional beliefs—even granting that those beliefs had a few difficulties that would have to be patched up. It was hard to "see" challenging information precisely because the old belief system provided a coherent picture of the world which *worked*. Likewise it is not comfortable for some of us, in the late twentieth century, to recognize the parochial nature of our prevailing belief system (even though it may seem to be based on the best science available). It is hard for us to "see" evidence that doesn't fit in, and that suggests the conventional worldview may be in a state of fundamental change. Despite our discomfort, it is essential to consider that possibility.

2

Recent conceptual developments in the mind-brain sciences rejecting reductionism and mechanistic determinism on the one side, and dualisms on the other, clear the way for a rational approach to the theory and prescription of values and to a natural fusion of science and religion.

—Roger Sperry

Consciousness
as
Causal Reality

It may seem strange that the consideration of consciousness as a "causal reality" is such an innovation. Doesn't it happen all the time, one wonders, that my *inner decision* to act *causes* something to happen in the objective world? Of course consciousness is a causal reality, one thinks. How could we have ever thought otherwise?

The Shaping of the Scientific Worldview

We need to recall how the science we know came into being. The modern worldview that began to take shape in the seventeenth century was the result of a revolt of what seemed to be common sense against a system of thought that had come to seem repugnant. It was a declaration of faith in the senses as opposed to the speculative mind, and in the visible world as opposed to the unseen. It emphasized the empirical (as a reaction against the authority of Scholasticism) and the reductionist (as a better explanation than the medieval "spiritual forces").

There were also ample grounds for separating the objective, which can be viewed by all, from the subjective, which is viewed in the privacy of one's own mind. There were good reasons to concentrate on the objective—one was simply that more rapid progress could be made, but an equally cogent one was avoiding a territorial clash with the institutions of religion. The early scientists could now explore anew such areas as astronomy, mechanics, and anatomy without confronting too directly the religious dogmas of the day, but to venture into the human mind—to deal with matters of personal human purpose, destiny, and will—was more hazardous.

Attempting to probe into the mind and spirit was also likely to feel inappropriate to the scientist himself. Many scientists (beginning with Descartes, a profoundly religious man) recognized the limited applicability of the new approach. They assumed a demarcation between those areas of human experience suitable for the scientific method because of their essentially impersonal and mechanical character and those not.

Thus the scientists felt free to devote themselves to their new exploration unencumbered by responsibility for the ultimates of existence, leaving that to theologians, philosophers, and poets. This division of realms gave the scientists a relatively free hand in physical discovery. It provided a respected barrier behind which they might conveniently pursue their research, untrammeled by the constraints of personal conscience and/or political and religious censorship.

Again we need to qualify the implication that the seventeenth century was a sharp watershed. History and social evolution do not come quite so neatly packaged nor proceed in such linear fashion. It appears that in the florescence of the Middle Ages, in the twelfth and thirteenth centuries, there was not only concentration on the spiritual and the hereafter, but also a keen interest in economic, political, and social matters which concern life on Earth. As early as the thirteenth century there was a blooming of invention in Western Europe, bringing forth such crucial developments as the iron axe and plow, the horsecollar, horseshoe, and stirrup, the windmill and waterwheel, and numerous craft techniques. For some reason, this technological impetus declined in the fourteenth and fifteenth centuries, and flowered again in the seventeenth and eighteenth centuries—the period we now think of as the beginning of the industrial revolution and the modern work ethic. Thus although the timing and form of the scientific revolution were indeed shaped by the evolution of the encompassing, broader society, the interaction of the two was complex.

By the nineteenth century science had expanded its activities into new areas of investigation, at the same time making increasingly exclusive claims for the cognitive. The scientific became equated with the reliably measurable, excluding a vast realm of human concern now discounted as "subjective" or "metaphysical".

In this regard the history of science is somewhat like the well-known story of the inebriate who had lost his housekey in the dark down the street and was searching for it under the corner streetlight because "the light is better here". For quite understandable reasons, in its early centuries the new search for truth called empirical science concentrated "where the light was better"—on exploration of the quantitatively measurable aspects of the physical environment, ignoring issues of the human mind and spirit central to the humanities and the religions. And because science was acquiring tremendous prestige, implication grew that there *was* nothing more to say. (It is as though the abovementioned searcher eventually came to conclude that there really isn't any street other than that area illuminated by the streetlamp.)

Every knowledge system is shaped by the characteristics of the society that produces it. We are accustomed to considering the flow in the opposite direction, seeing how scientific and technological advances have shaped modern society. But it is of critical importance to recognize both flows. We have the kind of society we have in part because of the fruits of science and technology. But the converse is also true: We have the kind of science we have in part because of the particular nature of the society in which it was developed.

Thus one way of viewing the scientific revolution is as a shift in the sort of knowledge that was valued by society. Medieval society was not strongly interested in technology. A new dynamism entered with the interrelated developments we call the Reformation, the rise of capitalism, and the scientific revolution. The underlying belief-system shift included increased emphasis on manipulation of the physical environment through technology. That in turn required a valuing of that knowledge which is useful for the development of technology—namely, knowledge that will enable prediction and control. Increasingly, through the first two-thirds of the twentieth century, scientific knowledge and the "scientific method" were identified with prediction-and-control knowledge. It went largely unnoticed that other societies (such as in ancient Greece, India, Europe in the Middle Ages) had valued other kinds of knowledge, useful for other purposes than the technological conquest of nature.

Another example of this shaping of science by society is seen in the current funding and support pattern. In the United States today, government funding of scientific research is, as a matter of policy, almost exclusively dedicated to pursuit of knowledge that will (a) aid the economy, (b) contribute to military technological capabilities, or (c) enhance medical high-technology. Other funding sources such as foundations are also strongly inclined in these directions.

In general, any society finds certain questions to be of great interest to it (such as, What knowledge will add to technological capability?), and others very much less so (for example, What kinds of inner exploration lead to a sense of deep meaning and purpose in life?). Thus *every society's knowledge system is parochial*—even modern science.

Furthermore, every lasting knowledge system satisfies the tests that it is put to. That is, human experience tends to confirm it, or it would not retain the commanding position that it holds. Thus there are cultures in which all of nature is alive and in communication with human beings, and there are cultures in which the weather, harvests, and game are managed by assorted gods. Whatever the belief system of a particular culture, it *works*. It has been subjected to tests, and reality is perceived as conforming to the belief system.

Part of the problem with the modern scientific worldview is that it hasn't worked in a critical area of individual and social life—the area of choosing and implementing fundamental value commitments. As Roger Sperry pointed out in his land-mark paper on "Changing Priorities":

> Beliefs concerning the ultimate purpose and meaning of life and the accompanying worldview perspectives that mold beliefs of right and wrong are critically dependent, directly or by implication, on concepts regarding the conscious self and the mind-brain relation and the kinds of life goals and cosmic views which these allow. Directly and indirectly social values depend . . . on whether consciousness is believed to be mortal, immortal, reincarnate, or cosmic . . . localized and brain-bound or essentially universal. . . . Recent conceptual developments in the mind-brain sciences rejecting reductionism and mechanistic determinism on the one side, and dualisms on the other, clear the way for a rational approach to the theory and prescription of values and to a natural fusion of science and religion.

Thus the Western neglect of the realm of subjective experience has had serious consequences in our confusion about values. For it is ultimately in this realm of the subjective, the transcendent, and the spiritual that all societies have found the basis for their deepest value commitments and sense of meaning.

Unspoken Assumptions of Conventional Science

It is humbling to the educated Westerner to realize that to an undeterminable extent science, like the traditional belief systems of "primitive" cultures, describes a world that is shaped by its built-in assumptions. To illustrate this, consider the following set of ten premises which, if encountered in a textbook a few decades ago, would hardly have aroused question:

A Rational Set of Premises for a Scientific Age

1. The only conceivable ways in which we can acquire knowledge are through our physical senses, and perhaps by some sort of information transmission through the genes. The sole way in which we extend our understanding of the

nature of the universe is through empirical science—that is, the exploration of the measurable world through instrumentation which augments our physical senses.

2. All qualitative properties (at least the ones we can talk about scientifically) are ultimately reducible to quantitative ones (for example, color is reduced to wavelength, thought to measurable brain waves, hate and love to the chemical composition of glandular secretions).

3. There is a clear demarcation between the objective world, which can be perceived by anyone, and subjective experience which is perceived by the individual alone, in the privacy of his/her own mind. Scientific knowledge deals with the former; the latter may be important to the individual, but its exploration does not lead to the same kind of publicly verifiable knowledge.

4. The concept of free will is a prescientific attempt to explain behavior which scientific analysis reveals is due to a combination of forces impinging on the individual from the outside, together with pressures and tensions internal to the organism.

5. What we know as consciousness or awareness of our thoughts and feelings is a secondary phenomenon arising from physical and biochemical processes in the brain.

6. What we know as memory is strictly a matter of stored data in the central nervous system, somewhat analogous to the storage of information in a digital computer.

7. The nature of time being what it is, there is obviously no way in which we can obtain knowledge of future events, other than by rational prediction from known causes and past regularities.

8. Since mental activity is simply a matter of dynamically varying states in the physical organism (primarily in the

brain), it is completely impossible for this mental activity to exert any effect directly on the physical world outside the organism.

9. The evolution of the universe and of man has come about through physical causes (such as random mutation, natural selection), and there is no justification for any concept of universal purpose in this evolution, or in the development of consciousness, or in the strivings of the individual.

10. Individual consciousness does not survive the death of the organism; or if there is any meaningful sense in which the individual consciousness persists after the death of the physical body we can neither comprehend it in this life nor in any way obtain knowledge about it.

Scanning the scientific and philosophical literature of the earlier part of the century, one can find endless statements confirming that the above premises are not an exaggeration of the the assumptions typically held. For instance:

Chemistry and physics account for so much of what the cell does, and for so much to which years ago physical science could at that time offer no clue, that it is justifiable to suppose that the still unexplained residue of the cell's behavior (and hence, man's behavior) will prove resolvable by chemistry and physics.
—Sir Charles S. Sherrington, physiologist

The hypothesis that man is not free is essential to the application of scientific method to the study of human behavior. The free inner man who is held responsible for the behavior of the external biological organism is only a prescientific substitute for the kinds of causes which are discovered in the course of a scientific analysis. . . . Science insists that action is initiated by forces impinging upon the individual, and that [freedom] is only another name for the behavior for which we have not yet found a cause.

—B. F. Skinner, psychologist

That man is the product of causes which had no prevision of the end they were achieving; that his origin, his growth, his hopes and fears, his loves and beliefs, are but the outcome of accidental collocations of atoms; that no fire, no heroism, no intensity of thought and feeling, can preserve an individual life beyond the grave; that all the labours of the ages, all the devotion, all the inspiration, all the noonday brightness of human genius, are destined to extinction in the vast death of the solar system, and the whole temple of Man's achievement must inevitably be buried beneath the debris of a universe in ruins—all these things, if not quite beyond dispute, are yet so nearly certain, that no philosophy which rejects them can hope to stand.

—Bertrand Russell, philosopher

In science we have to act as if the mechanistic theory of life were true, but we are in no way committed to it as a metaphysically valid statement. . . . Scientific progress can be made only by those who experiment as if mechanism is true.

—Joseph Needham, biologist

The child derives his identity from a social environment. The social environment remains to his death the only source for validating that identity. . . . The remarkable convergence of twentieth-century thinkers . . . is the elaboration of the idea that human meaning is arbitrary. . . . The world of human aspiration is fundamentally fictitious. If we do not understand this, we understand nothing about man.

—Ernest Becker, philosopher

On the other hand, the ten assumptions just listed would seem totally alien to any other than modern Western culture. Furthermore there is, in anecdotal accounts and in the existing research on consciousness and exceptional capabilities, an impressive amount of evidence that seems to contradict each of the premises listed.

Yet it was essentially on the basis of such assumptions that the increasingly prestigious scientific worldview was able, in the past, to dismiss as of secondary consequence the spiritual, aesthetic, and intuitive experiences of humankind, and hence to discredit value systems based in those subjective experiences.

However, as we have seen, it is well established from research in hypnosis and other areas of experimental psychology that once a person has an internalized picture of reality, further experience tends to confirm that picture. Reality is experienced in accordance with the established picture, sometimes at the cost of gross perceptual distortion and elaborate rationalization to make it all hold together. For example, it has been demonstrated over and over that the hypnotized subject not only sees reality in accordance with the internalized suggestions, but has very logical-sounding explanations as to why reality "really" is that way. Research on authoritarianism and prejudice shows clearly that people of a certain ethnic origin tend to be seen as having characteristics expected of that ethnic group. The Polish anthropologist Bronislaw Malinowski observed that the Trobriand Islanders, who believed that all characteristics are inherited from the father, regularly failed to see the child's resemblances to members of the mother's family. Anecdotal accounts in psychotherapy give countless examples of patients' rationalizing their obsessive-compulsive behavior.

Thus, to summarize again, we see the very important dual relationship between the experienced world and the science that is developed. The scientific knowledge that has been gained influences the way we perceive the world. *But*, the way the world is experienced in a particular culture influences what kind of science gets developed by that society.

Choose Your Metaphysic

That a society's basic experiencing of reality shapes its science, as well as the reverse, may be a profoundly disturbing thought if one pursues its implications. We who have been educated in modern society naturally assume that our scientific view of reality is essentially correct and other "prescientific" or "primitive" views are wrong. But we have to consider the possibility that some of those other views are seen through other cultural windows, and emphasize other aspects of the total human experience; they are not so much wrong as complementary. There is also the possibility that some sort of "transmodern" view in the future may be quite different from our own—and equally correct.

Improbable as it may seem to many, we appear to be going through another such profound change. Again at the heart of it is a challenge to the prevailing knowledge authority system. So far, the evidence for this sea change is scanty. We can invite the reader to observe the pattern; we cannot claim it is demonstrable.

Oversimplifying somewhat for clarity, let us think in terms of three basically different kinds of implicit metaphysic:

• **M-1.** In the first of these, the basic stuff of the universe is matter-energy. We learn about reality from studying the measurable world. (The positivist assumption is that that is the only way we can learn.) Whatever consciousness is, it emerges out of matter (that is, the brain) when the evolutionary process has progressed sufficiently far. Whatever we can learn about consciousness must ultimately be reconciled with the kind of knowledge we get from studying the physical brain, for consciousness apart from a living physical organism is not only unknown, it is inconceivable.

• **M-2.** An alternate metaphysic is dualistic. There are two fundamentally different kinds of basic stuff in the universe: matter-energy stuff and mind-spirit stuff. Matter-energy stuff is studied with the present tools of science; mind-spirit stuff must be explored in other ways more appropriate to it (such as inner, subjective exploration). Thus there develop, in essence, two complementary kinds of knowledge; presumably there are areas of overlap (such as the field of psychic phenomena).

• **M-3.** Yet a third metaphysic finds the ultimate stuff of the universe to be consciousness. Mind or consciousness is primary, and matter-energy arises in some sense out of mind. The physical world is to the greater mind as a dream image is to the individual mind. Ultimately the reality behind the phenomenal world is contacted, not through the physical senses, but through the deep intuition. Consciousness is not the end-product of material evolution; rather, consciousness was here first!

These three basic metaphysical perspectives are summarized briefly in the following table:

THREE METAPHYSICAL PERSPECTIVES

• M-1 MATERIALISTIC MONISM
(Matter giving rise to mind)

• M-2 DUALISM
(Matter plus mind)

• M-3 TRANSCENDENTAL MONISM
(Mind giving rise to matter)

The fundamental change which we are suggesting is happening in Western society can be put in terms of these metaphysics. Essentially, it is a shift of dominant metaphysic from M-1 to M-3. At first thought this may seem as outrageous a proposition as the heliocentric universe did to many in early seventeenth-century Europe. M-3 seems quite foreign to the Western mind, or certainly would have a generation ago. (It is not nearly so alien as it was even a quarter of a century ago, if we may judge from increased overt interest in the Eastern philosophical religions; purchases of books based around some sort of transcendental theme; appearances of "metaphysical" and Eastern transcendental concepts, such as reincarnation, karma, life-changing near-death experiences, in motion picture themes and innuendos; participation in meditative practices, workshops and seminars; widespread interest in the phenomenon of "channeling"; and other indicators.)

Although Descartes postulated a dualistic universe, by the twentieth century science was rather firmly committed to an M-1 metaphysic. Within the past decade or so some scientists, recognizing that the extreme positivist position simply doesn't square with human experience, have been writing and speaking about the need to re-base science on an M-2 metaphysic. (Nobel laureate Sir John Eccles is one example.) Quietly, a number of scientists find that when they take their total experience into account the M-3 metaphysic fits best; besides, that seems to be implicit in the esoteric "perennial wisdom" of the world's spiritual traditions. For the present, that position seems a long way from the picture of the world that emerges out of our various sciences. (However in the long run it may very well be where science ends up—but that is a point to be explored more fully in a later chapter.)

The above trichotomy, with its accompanying discussion, is deliberately somewhat oversimplified in the interest of clarity. A number of variants of these three metaphysical assumptions are preferred by one or another philosopher or scientist. For example, Roger Sperry espouses a position he calls *mentalism*, which we might designate M-1a. The mentalist concept assumes mind (that is, mental phenomena) to be emergent in the material evolution of the brain, not in any sense prior to the development of very complex neural circuitry. Once it is present, however, it makes possible a kind of "downward causation" (subjective mental state affecting physiological phenomena, for example). This is to be contrasted with the "upward causation" assumed throughout most science (for example, chemical changes in the body causing a subjective state). Another position, which we might term M-1b, is called *panpsychism*, and is much discussed in "post-modern" thought. This is the assumption that besides the physically observable properties of matter there has always existed an "inside aspect" of matter which resembles mind.

We should recognize that although science in its present form essentially evolved within an M-1 weltanschauung, it is perfectly compatible with either the M-2 or M-3 metaphysic. It is compatible, but in those views it is found to be inherently incomplete as a picture of the universe.

It is furthermore critically important to recognize that one does not set out to *prove* the validity of a metaphysic. Reality is far too rich to be adequately captured in any conceptualization of it—any conceptualization whatever. We are potentially capable of understanding aspects of reality that can never be adequately expressed in exact verbal form. It is not an appropriate question, then, to ask: Which of these three metaphysics is *true*? It *is* appropriate to ask: Which one seems to make the best fit with the *totality* of human experience?

The Plausibility of M-3 Dominance

This is indeed a bold claim we are making, namely that the M-1 dominance is declining, and the M-3 metaphysic is on its way to becoming the dominant metaphysic not only of this society, but of most of the world as well. The fact that no such fundamental change has occurred in Western society since the Copernican revolution, nearly four centuries ago, suggests the aptness of the phrase "the second Copernican revolution". Whereas the original Copernican revolution reordered our concepts of outer space, this one is concerned with our understanding of *inner* space.

First of all we should note that the M-3 orientation is by no means new in human history. As we shall show in more detail in Chapter 4, for thousands of years it has been part of the esoteric, inner-circle understanding, or *gnosis*, in most of the world's spiritual traditions. So also has been the concept of a cultural hypnosis which, although it differs in specific content from one culture to another, nevertheless tends to conceal an inner understanding that is akin to what we termed M-3. Throughout Western (and Eastern) cultural history there has been an esoteric tradition of the potentiality for the individual to become "dehypnotized" or "enlightened". A few quotations will serve as reminder of this fact:

In the ordinary waking state . . . man does not see the real world. . . . He lives in hypnotic sleep. . . . 'To awaken' for man means to be 'dehypnotized'.

—P. D. Ouspensky, *In Search of the Miraculous*

Humanity is asleep, concerned only with what is useless, living in a wrong world.

—Sanai of Afghanistan, AD 1130

Our conscious thinking has all the characteristics of a dream. . . . The representation that it gives us of the world is illusory. . . . In [a higher awareness state] consciousness is awakened in a way which is no longer exclusive or attached . . . it is liberated from usual hypnosis.

—Hubert Benoit, Zen scholar

We do not want to attain truth. We do not want anyone to break our dream.

—Swami Vivekananda

How are we to think of physical reality, then? The dream analogy, already mentioned briefly, is a good place to start. When we dream, there is typically a "story line"—events happen, and there seen to be some sorts of causal relations among them. While we are dreaming, everything in the dream seems real enough. When we awaken, we recognize that what felt so real was actually a dream. The law of causality is other than it seemed to be when we were asleep. In the dream it may have seemed that one event was the cause of something else, and so on. To the awakened self it is apparent that "I, the dreamer" am cause of the dream—events, interrelationships, and all.

Now try to imagine the analogue. In our ordinary state the world seems real; various kinds of events take place, and there are apparent causal relationships among them. Some of these relationships are so dependable, in fact, that we discover "scientific laws" to describe them. (Only rarely does mind seem to intrude in the physical world in such a way that anomalous phenomena occur.) But suppose one "awakens" from the "dream" of the physical world. It then becomes apparent that the causality law is different than we thought (and were taught): "I, the dreamer" (or "We, the collective dreamer") am the cause of the events and the relationships. The out-of-consciousness collective/universal mind is creator of the world which the conscious individual mind experiences.

This way of looking at reality must seem so strange to the Western educated mind that it is hard to take it seriously. In fact, although it may seem to be more characteristic of the Eastern philosophies, it is also present in the Western traditions and, as we have seen, it does not necessarily contradict the usual scientific view.

Remember, we are not arguing here that the M-3 metaphysic is *true*. We are merely trying to understand how it might be that some people—including some with rather sophisticated educational training—could have come to conclude that this way of seeing the world is more congenial to the totality of human experience than is the positivistic, reductionistic scientific worldview.

Most of the rest of this book will be directed toward examining some of the areas of human experience that seem to suggest the M-3 metaphysic, and exploring the implications for society if indeed it comes to predominate.

3

Unless there is a gigantic conspiracy involving . . . highly respected scientists in various fields, many of them originally hostile to the claims of the psychic researchers, the only conclusion the unbiased observer can come to must be that there are people who obtain knowledge existing in other people's minds, or in the outer world, by means yet unknown to science.

—H. J. Eysenck

Challenges
to Positivism
and
Reductionism

There are some areas, such as the ones we will explore in this chapter, which cannot be studied properly in the context of a science based on an M-1 metaphysic because positivism and reductionism don't seem to fit them. It is by no means clear what some future science based on an M-3 metaphysic might be like, but surely such a science will handle these areas more adequately.

The Mind in Health, Illness and Healing

Let us start with health, illness and healing. One of the most marvelous characteristics of the human organism is its ability to protect and maintain its health. In general, when we fall ill it is because this capability has been interfered with—and the chief interfering agent is the state of mind.

Essentially, each of us relies on three complex and highly interconnected bodily systems to maintain our well-being—the nervous system, the stress response system, and the immune system. The nervous system consists of the brain, the spinal cord, and the nerve pathways that extend to all parts of the body. It is the communication and command network for both external and internal changes, and the regulator of external and internal responses.

The nervous system has as subsystems the voluntary nervous system and the autonomic nervous system. The latter has two basic operating modes called the sympathetic and parasympathetic responses. The parasympathetic response is a condition of rest, relaxation, healing, and physical repair and regeneration. Food is digested, muscles relax and replenish energy supplies, tissues regenerate, all without attention from the conscious mind. The sympathetic response, in contrast, is a pattern of general alarm, arousal, and readiness to operate physically against external threat or dangers to the body. The sympathetic response (also called the fight-flight reaction) is triggered instinctively (unconsciously), without conscious direction. It typically is accompanied by (or evoked by) emotions of rage or fear. Its actions on the body may include acceleration of the heart rate, increased force of contraction of the heart, increased blood pressure and respiratory rate, shunting of blood supply from the inner organs to the muscles, secretion of sweat, dilation of the pupils, and other preparations for the intense activity involved in offense, defense, or escape.

The response of the sympathetic nervous system is one of the triggers of the second self-protective system, the stress response. The "hardware" of the stress-response system consists of the hypothalamus, pituitary, adrenal, and other glands, about a dozen or so in all, which together make up the endocrine system. (Stress response is only one of the functions of the endocrine system, which also has a number of regulatory and integrative functions in the body.) The stress-response system responds to external or internal sources of stress with a wide range of protective, regenerative, self-protective reactions, all of which are regulated by free-circulating body chemicals called hormones. For example, strong emotion associated with perception of a life-threatening situation results in several glands of the endocrine system releasing specific hormones into the bloodstream. This in turn increases the rate and force of contraction of the heart and constricts the peripheral blood vessels, thus raising blood pressure and circulation; dilates the bronchioles, aiding respiration; dilates the eye pupils for better vision; and increases the blood clotting ability to handle a potential injury. These effects help prepare the organism for either fight or flight.

The third self-protective bodily network is the immune system. This system is quite decentralized, and involves the white blood cells (leucocytes), the circulatory system, the lymphatic system, and certain glands and specialized areas. The key actors in it are about a trillion (10^{12}) lymphocytes (a form of white blood cell) and about 100 million trillion (10^{20}) molecules called antibodies that are produced and secreted by the lymphocytes. These comprise a sort of internal army that searches out and destroys invaders and enemies which break through the skin or enter the body from the air or in food. (Were the immune system to suddenly cease functioning, the microbes in the body would cause it to putrefy as rapidly as it would when kept in a warm environment after death.)

When activated, the immune system sends various protective cells and substances through the bloodstream and via the internal conduits of the lymph system, rushing to the site of the danger—an infection, puncture, cancer cell, or foreign body, for example. Multiplying rates of the white blood cells go up to replace those that may be lost in battle. Certain white cells (B-lymphocytes) manufacture specific substances (antibodies) which can attack and destroy the particular invader. (Because there are millions of different types of possible invaders, and because the antibodies are so specific to the foreign entities, there must be millions of different types of antibodies—and the right ones must be produced to attack the specific invaders.) Other actors in the system repair the damage and scan for further injury.

It has recently been discovered that these three systems—the central nervous system, the hormonal system, and the immune system—communicate with one another through "molecular messengers" called neuropeptides. "Messages" can originate in any part of the body; it appears that emotions and mental activity are far less centralized in the brain than used to be thought.

Good health depends upon the coordinated, constant effort of all three of these systems. Each of them can function perfectly well without conscious effort on our part. When the systems malfunction, we become ill. The role of the mind in creating illness has been increasingly appreciated as psychosomatic disorders and stress have become better understood.

For example, stress is our psychophysical response to *perceived* external changes and difficulties. Excessive or misplaced reaction to these external stressors takes a severe physiological toll on the body over time, and in the presence of an existing weakness in part of the body can cause physical disease. It is now quite clear that attitudes leading to stress can be a causative factor in a wide variety of illnesses, including gastric and duodenal ulcers, cardiovascular disease, migraine and tension headaches, arthritis and asthma. Certain personality types are found to be predisposed to these stress disorders—in particular, cardiovascular disease. Stress disorders have long since replaced infectious diseases as the major health afflictions of modern society.

Stress also can interfere with the functioning of the body's immune system. If the immune system is not functioning well, it can fail to intercept disease-causing viruses or bacteria, and illness may result. Or, it can fail to ferret out and destroy cancer cells when they occur, resulting in malignancy that gets completely out of control. Yet other diseases occur when the body's ability to produce antibodies is impaired. Still other ailments called autoimmune diseases (such as rheumatoid arthritis and multiple sclerosis) result when the immune system inappropriately attacks its own body's cells. Again, patterns of attitudes—personality types—are found to differ in their susceptibility to immune system disorder, and to the diseases that result.

Scientific descriptions of these protective systems elaborate on the mechanisms in far greater detail than we have here. The more one learns about the complexities of, for instance, the immune system the more miraculous the picture appears, and the less the purely mechanistic picture "feels right". Critical questions go largely unanswered—for instance: How do all the separate parts of the system communicate and function together to detect the specific invaders, to create just the right kinds of antibodies, to kill off or incapacitate the attacking bodies, and to clean up the mess afterwards? How do thoughts in the mind translate into interferences with immune system functioning?

If the role of the mind in creating illness is amazing, the role of the mind in healing is no less so. One specific form of this interaction is known as the "placebo effect". The basic phenomenon appears to be akin to hypnosis. If a patient accepts the suggestion that an inert substance (for example, a sugar pill) is in fact a powerful remedy, the result may be a healing—clearly brought about by the patient's mind since there is no medical consequence from the inert substance itself.

A now-famous case was described a number of years ago by Dr. Philip West, one of the pioneer researchers of psychological factors in illness. He was treating a man with severe cancer, who begged to be given the experimental drug Krebiozen. At that time Krebiozen was being touted by its proponents as a miracle cancer cure. After only one dose of the drug, the patient's tumor masses "melted like snowballs on a hot stove". Whereas he had once needed an oxygen mask to breathe, he soon became so active that he even began piloting his own plane. Shortly thereafter, however, he read about studies indicating that Krebiozen was ineffective. His cancer began to spread again, and he was hospitalized. His doctor, reacting to this dramatic turn of events, decided to lie to the patient, telling him not to believe the studies, and promised treatment with a new, more potent Krebiozen. In fact, the man was given only water, but nevertheless his condition improved significantly. His recuperation continued until one day he read in an article that the American Medical Association and the Food and Drug Administration had conclusively proved the worthlessness of Krebiozen. He immediately suffered a relapse, and died several days later.

Regeneration is a phenomenon closely related to healing. A portion of the body is destroyed—a small wound, let us say. At the same time the immune system is cleaning up the wound, the rest of the body goes ahead with restoring the missing tissue. The right kinds of cells multiply and fill in the empty space, stopping when the area is restored to its original shape. The accelerated growth of tissue does not go on and on, ending up with an unsightly bulge of scar tissue; it "knows when to stop". Regeneration in humans is not as spectacular as in some non-mammalian creatures. We do not grow back an amputated leg, for example, as a lobster will grow back an amputated claw. Nonetheless, the central feature remains the same. There appears to be a stored pattern that governs the regenerative process. If our science is based in the M-1 metaphysic, the pattern "must" be stored physically, perhaps in the cells or in the central nervous system—and we strain to believe that it is so. If the dominating metaphysic is, instead, M-2 or M-3, then the pattern can be a thought or an image, something like the image in the mind of a sculptor before he creates his masterpiece.

Let us again insert the reminder: We are not suggesting that the phenomena of healing—or any other phenomena— *prove* the incorrectness of the M-1 metaphysic. The positivistic, reductionistic scientific paradigm can be strained to fit almost anything, much as the Ptolemaic picture could be strained to fit increasingly accurate astronomical measurements. Perhaps it is essentially an aesthetic sense that in the end opts for the metaphysic or conceptual framework that can be adapted to experience with the least strain.

Attention and Volition

The most recently dominant metaphor in cognitive science is that of information processing. Let Morton Hunt, in his popular summary of the area, *The Universe Within*, describe how consciousness is dealt with here: "What has seemed to philosophers to be mind—a different sort of stuff from the brain—is not a separate stuff at all, but a series of processes of immense complexity, the integration of millions or billions of neural events. We call some of these macroevents 'ideas', but they are actually sets of physical microevents—concatenations of impulses, coded and processed and stored in memory. . . . [The] mind is . . . the brain's total set of symbol manipulations. . . . Mind is to the brain as digestion is to the stomach: The brain is what *is*, the mind is what the brain *does*."

The contents of consciousness are "actually sets of physical microevents". One could hardly find a more concise statement of the positivistic and reductionistic assumptions. With our cultural conditioning it may sound like a perfectly reasonable thing to say—but it just doesn't feel like the whole story.

One of the most problematic aspects of human experience when viewed from the M-1 standpoint is *volition*. Nothing is more central to the sense of self than the experience of volition—of "I choose", "I decide". The apparent conflict between the sense of volition and the deterministic assumption of positivistic science is one of the oldest problems in psychology. "Does free will exist?" was a common formulation of the puzzle.

In the M-1 outlook free will does indeed seem to present a paradox. For if we assume the omnicompetence and determinism of science and the universality of physical laws, then free will would seem to be no more than the feeling associated with a determined action. That is to say, I act in a way determined by all the external and internal forces acting upon me, and feel that it is my choice to do so. If we thus take free will to be an illusion, then we would also have to abandon such concepts as liberty, moral action, rational behavior, and so on.

Now there is a meaningful sense in which the feeling of freely choosing can indeed be self-deception, and we need to distinguish that from the more fundamental puzzle. We have already noted that we seem to choose unconsciously as well as consciously. Thus when I rationally decide that it is a poor idea to leave uneaten food on my dinnerplate, that may in fact turn out to be a consequence of my having internalized the parental insistence that leaving food on my plate is *bad*. But it is one thing to recognize unconscious along with conscious choice. It is quite another to insist that both are illusory, and there is no such thing as a choosing self.

One observation has long bothered those who may have felt that science must be deterministic—that however well one may defend this position rationally it is impossible to behave as though it were true. However logically sound the deterministic hypothesis may be, it never *feels* true to life.

Sir John Eccles, in his book (with Sir Karl Popper) *The Self and Its Brain* (1977), refers to the work of H. H. Kornhuber to bring out an interesting feature of volition. Kornhuber discovered the existence of electrical potentials generated in the cerebral cortex following the occurrence of will to action and prior to the actual performance of motor activity. He consistently observed an interval of a fraction of a second between the conscious act of will and the activity resulting from it. During this brief interval there is an observable flurry of electrical potentials which quickly focus on the appropriate cerebral area to bring about the action desired. But the delay between willing and willed activity is quite measurable. Eccles observes, "We can regard these experiments as providing a convincing demonstration that voluntary movements can be freely initiated independently of any determining influences that are entirely within the neuronal machinery of the brain."

On the other hand, there appears to be some work with evoked potentials that indicates the contrary—namely, electrical potentials in the nervous system that appear before the individual is consciously aware of having decided to act. Then there are those emergency situations where one responds instantaneously with a corrective or preventive action, and only afterward is aware of having made the right action decision "instinctively". Whatever may turn out to be the best way to understand volition, fitting it into the M-1 metaphysic remains a strain.

Let us look at one rather well-known experiment by hypnosis researcher Ernest Hilgard that bears on the question: Who is choosing? A subject was hypnotized and told that his left (nonwriting) hand would feel no pain. He was then instructed to place that hand in a container of ice-cold water and ice cubes. Although this would normally be quite painful, the subject reported—as expected—that he felt quite comfortable. Meanwhile, the subject was asked to engage in "automatic writing" with his right hand—to simply let the hand write "anything it wanted to" without the subject's paying any particular attention to it. After several minutes, when asked how his immersed hand felt, the subject replied that it was fine. At the same time, however, his other hand was complaining bitterly by writing such things as "it hurts" and "ouch". Thus one part of the psyche (including the conscious, reporting mind) is unaware of the pain, while another part is experiencing it and giving expression to it. This "other part of the psyche" Hilgard terms the "hidden observer".

Volition is obviously not a simple matter. Closely related to this phenomenon is that of attention. Sitting in my study I can pay attention to what I am reading. Alternatively, my mind can wander to something that happened yesterday; or I can pay attention to whether my body is comfortable—free from itches, aches, and the like; or I may shift my attention to a noise that has been present, unobtrusively, while I was reading.

Attention is more important than it may first appear to be, for how I attend will affect what I perceive, and what I perceive will affect how I interpret my experience. If I listen to a person's words I may have a very different interpretation of a conversation than if I attend to the person's body language and observe the subtle messages that come to me from shifty eyes, posture and gestures.

But with attention as with volition, we have an everyday phenomenon that fits only with great strain into an M-1 worldview. Who is the self that chooses? Who is the self that attends?

Mind, Instinct and Evolution

The complex instinctual behaviors of animals is another area that raises similar questions. Myriad examples could be brought forth; let us take one cited by Rupert Sheldrake in his book *A New Science of Life*.

The European cuckoo lays its eggs in the nests of birds of other species. The young, hatched and reared by these unwitting foster parents, never see their real parents. Towards the end of the summer, the adult cuckoos migrate to their winter habitat in southern Africa. About a month later, the young cuckoos congregate and then they also migrate to the same region of Africa. where they join their elders. They instinctively know that they should migrate and when to migrate; they instinctively recognize other young cuckoos and gather together; and they instinctively know in which direction they should fly and what their destination is.

Do the cuckoos have some elaborate computer-like program stored in their genes? The answer of M-1 science tends to be "It must be so". Or do the young cuckoos tune in to the Great Cuckoo Mind in the Sky and take their directions from there? It sounds absurd, yet something like that is what Sheldrake suggests with his concept of "formative causation".

According to this concept, systems are organized in the way they are now because similar systems were organized that way in the past. The characteristic behaviors of biological organisms are influenced by invisible organizing fields operating across space and time. These hypothesized *morphogenetic fields* are a sort of cumulative record of past behaviors, weighted in favor of those behaviors that worked for the species—in somewhat the same sense as natural selection. Thus, for instance, the spider learns to spin and repair a web—not through imitating its parents, nor from some genetic programming, but from the nonmeasurable cumulative morphogenetic field that contains the trial-and-error learning of all generations past.

One of the examples offered by Sheldrake involves a series of experiments carried out by Harvard psychologist William McDougall in the early 1920s, aimed at testing whether learned behavior patterns are inherited. McDougall placed rats in a specially constructed water tank from which they could escape by swimming to an unlighted gangway. If, instead, a rat swam to a brightly lighted gangway, it would receive an electric shock. The rats' rates of learning were measured by counting the number of errors they made before learning to swim straight to the unlighted gangway. Quite surprisingly, it turned out that later generations of rats learned more rapidly than the generations preceding them. The experiment was continued for 32 generations and took 15 years to complete. From first to last generations of rats there was over a tenfold increase in their rate of learning. Much more surprisingly, when separate studies in Scotland and Australia were designed to replicate McDougall's experiments, the first generation of rats learned almost as rapidly as McDougall's 32nd generation. A number of the rats even "learned" the task immediately, without making a single error.

These results are completely inexplicable in conventional terms. Not only is learned behavior not supposed to be inherited, there is no way of accounting for transmission of learning between completely isolated groups of rats. The Sheldrake concept of accounting for behavior patterns through a cumulative nonphysical morphogenetic field, not spatially confined, fits the observed results easily. This idea may seem in an M-1 frame of mind to be an outrageously wild hypothesis. But the concept does not seem so strange viewed from the standpoint of an M-2 or M-3 metaphysic, in which consciousness is not constrained to fit our usual physicalistic expectations.

Most scientists would agree that instinctual behaviors, whatever their origins, are among the characteristics that arise through the process of evolution and are genetically transmitted to each succeeding generation of the species.

The origin of the diverse forms of life on the Earth, as generally understood, is familiar enough in outline. Some fifteen billion years ago the present universe began, with the "Big Bang". Around three billion years ago the first life appeared on the Earth; and two-tenths of a billion years ago, the first mammals. Although some aspects of the origin of life remain uncertain, scientists ordinarily assume it came about through some sort of chance combining of nucleic acids and proteins. Thereafter, more and more different forms of life appeared, essentially through the process of random mutation and natural selection. Along this evolutionary path there evolved the attribute of mind or consciousness. (Nonmaterial consciousness is assumed to appear out of a material world—a world of matter and energy. As we saw earlier, one attempt to deal with this paradox is to argue that the mind is simply process—it is "what the brain does".)

Darwin's theory of evolution is essentially based in a very few assumptions. One of the most central is that there is a continual struggle for survival, in which the great majority of contestants lose. Another is that there is a natural range of variation in all species, both in trivial traits and in essential ones. In highly competitive organisms, some of these variations must confer an advantage or a disadvantage in the struggle for the means of survival. Thus there is a natural selection, whereby organisms which are less well fitted to their conditions of life tend to be eliminated, while those which are better fitted are more likely to survive and to leave progeny. The result is a gradual modification of species in the direction of greater adaptedness.

The main source of variation within organisms of the same species is now known to be mutations of the genetic material, the genes based on deoxyribonucleic acid (DNA). Mutations are small changes in the molecular structure of the DNA that arise as a consequence of some damaging chemical or radiation, and are essentially random.

A number of challenges have been put to the neo-Darwinist evolutionary hypothesis (that is, the Darwinist theory modified by what has since been learned about the genetic mechanisms of inheritance). One of these challenges is the Lamarckian concept of inheritance of acquired or learned characteristics. (This was the hypothesis McDougall was testing in the experiments just described.) In the sense of acquired characteristics being genetically transmitted to succeeding generations, this hypothesis is generally discarded. However, in the sense of the cumulative learning of the species being somehow preserved in the morphogenetic field, as proposed by Sheldrake, the idea may be showing signs of revitalization.

Another challenge has been to the assumption that gradual transformation involving small changes each generation could account for the tremendous diversity of organisms existing on the Earth. Apart from anything else, the organisms differ in the number and structure of their chromosomes, so that some more abrupt and major changes must have occurred.

Most puzzling of all in the neo-Darwinist conceptualization of the evolutionary path is the appearance of complex structures and behaviors that seem to have survival value only in the final form, not in intermediate stages. An often-cited example is binocular vision. Binocular vision is found in mammals and many other creatures. The eye itself is an exquisitely designed instrument for visual perception; the binocular feature using two eyes gives added depth perception. Once the two eyes are present it is easy enough to see their survival value. But how can we imagine a gradual evolvement of binocular vision in tiny stages, each step a result of random mutation, and each step having sufficient survival value so that it is favored as the characteristics are passed on to successive generations? Or alternatively, can we imagine the accidental appearance of an organism which in one leap arrives at rudimentary binocular vision with sufficient survival value that through successive generations of natural selection it gets perfected to the present form? Although such kinds of explanation leave a tremendous lot to "accident", they are nonetheless the preferred form of explanation in a science committed to an M-1 metaphysic.

Consider another kind of explanation which speaks of some sort of teleological "pull" in the evolutionary process, of evolution toward increased awareness, complexity, freedom—in short, of evolution *going somewhere* (not in a predetermined sense, but in the sense of preferred direction). In that kind of evolutionary explanation the organism developed two eyes because at some deep level of inner understanding it wanted to see better! Perhaps a species on the long path of evolutionary development is not only pushed by random mutations and natural selection, but also pulled by the kind of teleological force implied in Henri Bergson's *Creative Evolution* and much more forthrightly in Teilhard de Chardin's *The Phenomenon of Man*. In this kind of explanation *mind is prior to brain*, and evolution is characterized both by the organism's freedom to choose and by its inner sense of "right" direction. This has been a totally unacceptable form of explanation in modern scientific debate—yet it is much more congenial to the emerging view that consciousness has somehow to be factored into our total scientific picture of the universe.

Exceptional Capabilities

Throughout all the debates pertaining to the limitations of M-1 science there is one area that has generated the most heated controversy of all—the area of exceptional capabilities, particularly those which seem in some way to contradict the basic scientific picture of reality. In Chapter 2 we listed ten tacit assumptions of conventional science. We refer now to capabilities and phenomena which appear to challenge one or more of those assumptions.

In Chapter 1 we mentioned one such phenomenon which has recently become in vogue as a powerful demonstration of the power of suggestion—firewalking. There have been many valiant attempts to somehow accommodate this experience to the M-1 metaphysic—insulating ash, insulating layer of steam, etc. Whatever intermediating mechanism one assumes, the fact of the matter appears to be that if one holds one's consciousness or attention one way the bare feet will quickly receive third-degree burns from the burning coals and if one holds the mind a different way the feet stay free from harm.

In all traditional societies stories are told of men and women with seemingly miraculous powers, and such powers are recognized by all religions. In many parts of the world various paranormal abilities are said to be cultivated deliberately within esoteric systems such as shamanism, sorcery, tantric yoga, and spiritualism. And even in modern Western society there are persistent reports of apparently inexplicable phenomena, such as telepathy, clairvoyance, precognition, memories of past lives, hauntings, poltergeists, psychokinesis, and so on.

The scientific study of allegedly paranormal phenomena has been going on for at least a century and a half, although it has seldom been wholeheartedly supported by the research establishments within which it was carried out. Although there have been some cases of fraud and delusion, and some supposedly paranormal events which turned out to have reasonable normal causes, a residue remains of occurrences which appear to defy explanation in terms of any known physical principles. Moreover, numerous experiments designed to test for so-called extrasensory perception or for psychokinesis have yielded results with the odds against chance explanation being millions to one and higher.

Insofar as these phenomena cannot be explained in terms of the known laws of physics and chemistry, from the standpoint of the M-1 metaphysical assumptions they ought not to happen. If they appear to occur nevertheless, then they depend either on laws of physics as yet unknown, or on non-physical causal factors or connecting principles.

One common classification of psychic phenomena is given below:

- *Extrasensory perception* (where information appears to be obtained under conditions which rule out the known sensory channels)

  Telepathy (in which this communication appears to be mind-to-mind)

  Clairvoyance (in which there appears to be direct apprehension of information that would not normally be assumed to be accessible—for example, the phenomenon of remote viewing)

  Precognition (in which one seems to have information regarding events that have not yet happened—sometimes occurring in the form of a "memory" of something happening some time *hence*)

  Retrocognition (in which there appears to be knowledge of, or "memory" of, events that happened in the past but which the person could not know about in ordinary ways)

- *Psychokinesis* (where the state of a person's mind appears to exert a direct effect on the physical environment)

  Simple psychokinesis (in which the state of mind apparently results in something being moved or physically affected at a distance and without physical intervention of the ordinary sort, for example, the reported metal-bending demonstrations)

  Levitation (of oneself)

  Teleportation (apparent disappearance of an object from one location and appearance at another)

  Materialization and *dematerialization*

  Thought photography (in which a held image or mental state apparently results in an image on photographic film)

  Psychic healing and *psychic surgery*

- *Mediumship or channeling* (apparent communication with discarnate beings, sometimes accompanied by physical or quasi-physical phenomena)

The healthy skeptic will be pretty certain that most of the types of phenomena listed could not occur at all, and the few that seem to will eventually be susceptible to "natural" and "scientific" explanations. Yet the plain fact of the matter is that (like firewalking) all of these have been reported in a variety of societies, over dozens of centuries, and all have been investigated by careful and scientifically sophisticated observers. That is not to say that they have been "demonstrated" to the satisfaction of the scientific community—far from it. To the contrary, the data remain tantalizingly equivocal (for reasons we shall explore in the next chapter). But all the same, when we take into account the potentiality of whole cultures to see "realities" that other cultures don't see, the experimental research on, and anecdotal reports of, psychic phenomena cannot be totally dismissed.

As H. J. Eysenck, head of the Department of Psychology at Maudsley Hospital in London, summed it up about thirty years ago, "Unless there is a gigantic conspiracy involving 30 university departments all over the world, and several hundred highly respected scientists in various fields, many of them originally hostile to the claims of the psychic researchers, the only conclusion the unbiased observer can come to must be that there are people who obtain knowledge existing in other people's minds, or in the outer world, by means yet unknown to science."

In the M-1 metaphysical assumption frame this is all totally baffling, and leads to a fruitless search for "physical mechanisms". From the M-2 viewpoint the occurrence of the phenomena is not so disturbing, but it is not obvious what kind of research will lead to understanding of the consistently inconsistent nature of the data.

In the M-3 framework the erratic nature of psychic phenomena tends to be understood as related to the psychological phenomenon of resistance. No such phenomena are intrinsically impossible, but they do violate the order that is (in a sense) "agreed upon" in the collective mind. Thus while such phenomena may occur on occasion, there is deep-level unconscious resistance to exactly the kind of data the scientist seeks— data that would "scientifically demonstrate" the existence of these anomalous events.

Of all the challenges to positivism and reductionism, these exceptional capabilities are the most directly challenging, the most elusive, and the most controversial.

4

*Truth is not that which is
demonstrable. Truth is that
which is ineluctable.*
                              —St. Exupery

The New Paradigm
in Psychology:
Legitimating the
Transpersonal

The fundamental puzzle of Western science has been long recognized. If the world that science tells us about is reality, how does it happen that we don't feel more at home in it? If my most direct experience of reality is my own conscious awareness, why doesn't science have more of a place for consciousness? Indeed, there have been attempts in the past to bring consciousness into a more central place in the knowledge system. Some of these (for example, phenomenology, introspectionism, gestalt) failed to gain acceptance as meeting basic methodological criteria; others (such as Tibetan Buddhist psychology) come from other cultures and are only now receiving serious consideration.

Once we recognize that bias is inevitable in any society's knowledge system (two of the main sources being the tacit metaphysical assumptions and the bias toward culturally useful knowledge), the question of how to test that knowledge becomes central. Testing scientific knowledge is a more subtle matter than is sometimes assumed. Two criteria are commonly taken to be most characteristic of the scientific method, namely, *objectivity in investigative procedures* and *reliability through replicable experiments*.

The Difficult Task of Being Open-minded

Let us consider objectivity. In the present context, the word means that one seeks to obtain a view of reality undistorted by personal feelings or prejudices. It thus implies not only research procedures that insulate the findings from the desires and expectations of the researcher, but also openness to new evidence that may force change in one's beliefs. Thus it is not just a characteristic of scientific methodology; it refers also to *a character trait of the investigator.*

There has been a tendency in teaching the history of scientific thought to represent the Scholastics of the Middle Ages as being congenitally closed to new thoughts. The scientist, on the other hand, is portrayed as ever curious after new facts and eager to have his theories demolished by the impact of new data—then reconstructed in ever more inclusive form. History records how the scientists Galileo and Bruno and Harvey were harassed and opposed by the established powers citing classical authority. We sometimes gloss over the harassment and opposition suffered by Semmelweis, Pasteur, Darwin, Freud, and numerous others, from their own scientific colleagues.

If one looks beneath the covers in the history of science, one sees no end of examples of ill treatment by scientists of other scientists whose theories or investigation didn't "fit in" with accepted conceptual frameworks. However, there is little point in criticizing these scientists who exhibit an all-too-human frailty. The conscious desire may well be to be open and objective; unconscious protectiveness may cause the behavior to be otherwise. We are not just referring to the scientist who has so much ego-involvement with his own theory that psychologically he can't afford to see conflicting evidence. Even more powerful and ubiquitous is the issue of being objective in the face of the unconscious assumptions shared by one's entire culture (or scientific subculture).

The early seventeenth-century authorities may not have been very open-minded about unexpected indications of satellites revolving around Jupiter. We may assume, however, that they were quite willing to investigate, within the approved framework of methodology, a claim of dream prophecy, of miraculous healing, of the appearance of a figure resembling the Virgin Mary, or of a meditating monk seemingly rising off the ground and being suspended in the air. Thus in an important way often neglected, *objectivity is a function of the prevailing (partly unconscious) assumptions about the nature of reality.*

One thinks, for example, of the pronouncements of the committee appointed by the French Academy in 1772 to investigate reports of what are now called meteorites—those extraterrestrial bodies that appear as flaming objects streaking through the sky and crash to the ground as scorched hunks of metal and stone. (The committee included Antoine Lavoisier, the "father of modern chemistry".) The conclusion reached by the committee, after long deliberations and examination of much evidence, was that with which they started: There are no such things as hot stones that have fallen from the sky because there are no stones in the sky to fall. The prevailing interpretation of the Newtonian model of the solar system left no room for these extraneous bodies. Therefore the reported phenomena must have other explanations—delusionary "visions", stones heated from being struck by lightning, stones borne aloft by whirlwinds or volcanic eruptions, etc. Such was the prestige of the committee and so convincing its arguments that museums all over Western Europe threw away their meteorite specimens. As a result, there are very few preserved meteorite specimens that date prior to 1790.

More recently, the fate of scientists who presumed to take seriously the persistent reports of unidentified flying objects (UFOs) has been harassment and ridicule. The basic argument seems to be that there is no way the phenomena could be accounted for within accepted conceptual frameworks; hence the thousands of investigated phenomena must not have occurred, the striking photographs of UFOs must all have been faked, and the corroborating data must be the product of some kind of conspiracy to deceive.

The history of the physics of light is interesting in this regard. As far back as 1650, the Italian physicist Francesco Grimaldi had performed some experiments, shining light through a narrow slit and obtaining a pattern of light and dark bands which we would now term a diffraction pattern. The work excited only short-lived interest, because of the general acceptance of Newton's views regarding the particle nature of light. Thomas Young's epoch-making 1802 papers which described experiments on interference, suggesting a wave-type theory, were called by a member of the Royal Society "paltry and unsubstantial papers . . . destitute of every species of merit". The abusive attack on Young marred his reputation for many years; feelings over the issue ran high. One critic warned that the wave theory "can have no other effect than to check the progress of science and renew all those wild phantoms of the imagination which . . . Newton put to flight from her temple".

In spite of such vehement opposition, the wave theory won a temporary victory. Discouragement and ridicule were now aimed at attempts, which started in the eighteenth century, to measure the pressure of light impinging on a solid body. The reason was because, as a priori reasoning argued, there was no conceivable way that nonmaterial waves could exert pressure. (Later on, as it turned out, the pressure of light was not only observed but fit into theory.) Maxwell's mathematical theories of electromagnetic waves initially met with widespread rejection because of the problem of imagining some sort of all-pervading "ether" to support the waves. To his dying day, Lord Kelvin never accepted Maxwell's hypotheses and insisted that Roentgen's discovery of X-rays (like light with extremely short wavelength) must be some sort of elaborate hoax—because a priori reasoning showed they couldn't exist. Meanwhile Einstein had proposed the photon or "light particle" theory of light, and its opponents were objecting that its acceptance would throw science back by centuries.

Bohr's complementarity principle finally furnished a resolution of the wave-particle controversy. In essence this principle asserts that the wave and particle descriptions represent complementary aspects of a reality which cannot be fully conceptualized in either metaphor alone. We are free to measure either the wavelength or the position of a photon as precisely as we choose. But the two quantities do not appear in the same conceptual model, and an attempt to think in terms of both at the same time leads to a paradoxical situation. For the principle of uncertainty states that the more precise our knowledge of the wavelength, the greater is our ignorance regarding the position, and vice-versa. That is, what is "real" in one model is elusive, if not illusory, in the other. (Note the intriguing similarity, in this respect, of the relationship between consciousness and matter-energy.)

Fashions change with regard to what kinds of explanations are acceptable. The sedative effect of opium was explained in pre-Newtonian days by the assumption that opium has a "dormitive potency". In the late seventeenth century, with the prevailing faith that all facets of physical experience could ultimately be expressed in terms of elementary particles, the favorite explanation for opium's sedating and analgesic qualities had it that the round shape of the opium molecules soothes the nerves along which they move. In our own day we are more likely to be comfortable accounting for pain suppression in speaking of opium molecules affecting the sleep center of the brain, and of the mating of endorphin-like molecules in the opiate with receptors in the central nervous system. But the situation has not changed essentially. We have no adequate conceptualization of the nature of sleep, or of sedation, or of pain and its relief—because we have no adequate conceptualization of the role of consciousness in these processes.

During the eighteenth century the Royal Society suppressed evidence supporting the existence of various phenomena of witchcraft. Later, similar evidence was recognized and studied—but as manifestations of hypnotic powers. Hypnosis itself was largely rejected by the early scientific community as "animal magnetism". (The investigating commission that concluded in 1784 that no "magnetic fluid" exists included Benjamin Franklin and Lavoisier. Striking recoveries from illnesses were not denied, but, rather, attributed to "mere imagination".) The first comprehensive delineation of hypnotic effects was put forth in 1826, and included amnesia, analgesia, hallucinatory activity, improved recall ability, hypersuggestibility and compliance, telepathic communication, "sight without eyes" (clairvoyant remote viewing), clairvoyant ability to diagnose, prescribe for and prognosticate about illness, and ability to take on the illnesses of other people and cure them.

Hypnosis tended to be a relatively taboo area for university research until the mid-twentieth century. This was undoubtedly true in part because of this early association with extrasensory perception. The definition no longer includes or implies such phenomena, and they are seldom reported in laboratory research. This may mean that they never occurred at all, or it may mean that their occurrence is precluded by the contemporary researcher's disbelief. (It is somewhat ironic that one of the foremost nineteenth-century researchers in extrasensory perception, F. W. H. Myers, complained that British research in telepathy was held up because of its association with the unsavory area of hypnosis!)

Around 1840 physicians John Elliotson in London and James Esdaile in Calcutta made extensive use of hypnotic suggestion to carry out painless major surgery, including leg amputations. Medical journals denied publication of the results on the grounds that there was no conceivable explanation for the claimed analgesic effects. Although hundreds of apparently painless major operations were performed, some in public demonstration, doctors and patients were accused of "deluding or colluding". Patients, it was claimed, must have been just pretending to feel no pain while they had legs amputated or abdominal operations performed without benefit of anesthetic!

We have earlier observed that parapsychology has been an extraordinarily controversial area throughout most of its century-long history. Attacks have ranged from quiet ridicule to open hostility. Critics tended to ignore the fact that data on the spontaneous occurrence of presumably paranormal phenomena had been carefully collected for decades prior to the initiation of serious efforts to conduct controlled experiments. They charged or hinted at faulty techniques in experimentation (failure to insure against sensory cues, systematic errors perhaps unconsciously influenced by the experimenter's bias in favor of the ESP hypothesis, erroneous use of statistical methods), at gullibility and at willful deception. By divide-and-demolish techniques, experimental findings were disposed of, one by one, on the multiple bases of chance, error, and fraud. At mid-century neurophysiologist D. O. Hebb typified the prevailing scientific opinion in admitting, "I do not accept ESP for a moment because it does not make sense. My external criteria, both of physics and of physiology, say that ESP is not a fact despite the evidence that has been reported." (More succinctly to the point was the remark of a well-known contemporary scientist who, when confronted with some particularly convincing evidence of clairvoyant remote-viewing, snorted, "I wouldn't believe it if it *were* true!")

We can easily see that some of the best scientists have had their difficulties with being objective. The problem is faced frontally in the case of dealing with self-reports of subjective experience, which is a key issue in consciousness research.

Scientific Objectivity and Reliability

Consider a common form of research—testing the efficacy of a new analgesic by giving the drug to a large population of subjects and making a statistical analysis of the data. Pain is a subjective response affected by all sorts of subtle variables, such as the subject's desire to cooperate with the experimenter, placebo effect, deliberate or inadvertent suppression of pain by autosuggestion, individual uniqueness, variability of the subject's responses from day to day. Even with all the sophistication of double-blind techniques, you would not expect, in research that so centrally involves self-reports of subjectively felt pain, to be able to apply rigid definitions of objectivity and of replicability. Nor would you expect that the merits of the research should be severely criticized because of this intrinsic difficulty.

In research more directly related to exploring the powers of mind, the problems with objectivity and replicability are more acute. Take two examples: research on imagery and suggestion as aids to cancer remission, and research on psychokinesis. In both cases there is a fair amount of careful work carried out by competent researchers; in both cases the results would strongly suggest the existence of a genuine phenomenon. Yet because of the absence of some sort of "mechanism" to account for the phenomenon, stringent demands are placed on the research findings—and by strict standards, they fail to pass the test. Researchers with positive beliefs about the phenomena tend to report positive results, and skeptics tend to get negative results—thus raising the question of objectivity. And the results are erratic even under what appear to be similar conditions.

The skeptical tend to interpret these characteristics of the research as evidence for the nonexistence of the phenomena; however, they can also be interpreted as indications of inappropriate demands for "objectivity" and "replicability" in an area of research where the usual meanings of the words don't fit. Once one postulates the possibility of the subject's mind affecting the environment at a distance, then it becomes apparent that the state of the experimenter's mind can also affect the results—so strict objectivity is an impossibility. Once we recognize that human beings make choices at unconscious as well as conscious levels (such as addiction—an unconscious choice overruling a conscious one; or guilt feeling—a message from part of the unconscious mind that it disapproves of a choice made consciously) then the phenomena must be reinterpreted. Unconscious as well as conscious choices are involved in either cancer healing or psychokinesis. The person may want one thing at a conscious level, yet unconsciously want its opposite. With this uncontrollable factor entering in, strict replicability is impossible.

Thus, rigid interpretations of objectivity and of reliability through replicability would appear to be inappropriate when the matter being researched involves consciousness and subjective experience. However, surely there are criteria something like these which *are* appropriate. For instance, the Buddhist ideal of *nonattachment* would come highly recommended as a substitute for objectivity. In the Buddhist tradition (which implies M-3 metaphysical assumptions) one's perception can be undistorted only when there is no attachment to theories, expectations, outcomes, desires, material rewards and such like.

As to reliability, if we are working in an area in which strict replicability of controlled experiments is not to be expected (or even, as in astronomical research, replicability of measurements on systems which one can neither perturb nor control), still there must be some way in which we assess the trustworthiness of knowledge. It may have to be established on the basis of multiple imperfect tests. (For example, scientists have often chosen between two theories both of which seem to fit with the known facts, on the basis of one being more aesthetically elegant than another.)

Multiple Persons in a Single Body

Research on multiple personalities is an interesting area that illustrates some of the difficulties associated with self-report data. The conscious "ordinary" self is usually quite sure of being one mind in one body. The self that dreams knows another world, but is also sure, both in the dream state and when awake, that it is the same "I". However there are persons— victims of "multiple personality disorder"—who appear to have two or more distinct personalities. (Dr. Jekyll and Mr. Hyde is the classic fictional example.) In actual cases the condition almost always seems to have its roots in severe child abuse, and is typically confusing and painful for the persons who suffer from it. Current research on this phenomenon is interesting from a number of standpoints, including some methodological puzzles.

In such a person (a "multiple"), different personalities (which in many cases have no awareness of one another) alternately control the physical body. Alternate personalities may be quite dissimilar in speech and thought patterns, mood, temperament, voice characteristics, apparent gender, physiognomy, posture and movement patterns, accessible memories, reported age and life history, and other individual and personality characteristics. Different personalities have often mastered different physical abilities, interpersonal skills, and intellectual subject areas. They may be able to speak different foreign languages. The impression that wholly different personalities are expressing themselves through a single body can be corroborated by correlating these various changes with the personality shifts as subjectively experienced by the psychiatrist or researcher.

The current surge of research interest in this topic has come about partly because of the discovery that in these cases of personality shift, physiological and biochemical changes may be observed as well. These can include brainwave patterns, chemical composition of bodily fluids, immune status, allergies, skin electrical responses, and others. This development leaves little doubt that in some important sense the alternate personality "really exists" as surely as does the usual personality. Research on multiples could potentially shed new light on a host of questions relating to consciousness.

The study of multiple personalities raises a different sort of methodological question. Most of conventional science seeks reductionistic explanations for phenomena. But "personality", like "health" and "love", is a holistic concept. How is truth sought in an area where one has to deal with a holistic situation that includes not only behavior and other measurable dimensions, but also the full spectrum of subjective experience? The most fruitful inquiry appears to involve explorations of these inner experiences, often quite profound and moving, in an atmosphere of mutual trust and rapport—not at all like the cold detachment of the controlled experiment.

Switching from one personality to another may be a voluntary act on the part of the multiple, or it may be spontaneous—often triggered by emotional response to a situation. Some alternate personalities appear to be destructive; they may be masochistic, or get the multiple in trouble through sociopathic behavior. Sometimes an alternate has a role as helper. One personality may exhibit unusual physical strength, and act as protector when the situation requires physical protection. Another may act as healer, and take over in emergencies with extraordinary knowledge about how to heal the body. An alternate may take over the body while the main personality is "sleeping", and prepare dinner, clean up the dishes, or perform other helpful acts. When one personality is stressed or tired, another may take over and function at a high level of effectiveness.

Under some conditions alternates may permanently "fuse" into a single personality, or alternate personalities may "leave". Both of these events can lead to more comfort for the patient, and higher levels of effectiveness; in other words, they may be part of a "cure". But in the rare case a multiple doesn't want to be "cured"; having the body run by a well-functioning committee, so to speak, may be handier than being limited to one personality.

In the course of therapy one particular alternate may be encountered, which has been termed the "inner self helper". This unique personality is typically very cooperative with the therapist, even to the point of giving advice and pointing out mistakes. It seems to never display negative emotions such as hatred, anger, anxiety, fear, depression. It is typically cheerful and loving, with a good sense of humor. It seems to be both wise and compassionate. This "helper" personality appears to be potentially present in every known case, although it may not appear spontaneously. Unlike the other alternates, who typically report having been "born" during some traumatic period in the early childhood of the body, this particular one is likely to say, "I have always been". Queried about death, it reports that at death the body decays and the other personalities disintegrate, but "I remain". (It is interesting to compare this recent finding with the following quotation from the *Upanishads* [India, 1000 BC]: "The *atman*, the Self, is never born and never dies. . . . It is beyond time, unborn, permanent, and eternal. It does not die when the body dies.")

The phenomenon of multiple personalities seems related to other kinds of dissociative states, some of which are not considered pathological but, rather, highly prized. Of course we all have alternate personalities in a sense; we have each experienced periods when we definitely feel the internalized parent to be in control, or the petulant child. One dissociative experience often considered to be beneficial is called out-of-body experience; it is sometimes associated with a near-death episode. Many persons have reported that such an experience has had a positive, transformative effect on their lives. Another example is the subjective experience of some sort of inner genius, such as the poet's muse or Socrates' "daemon", that may present an answer to a question, the solution to a problem, or a musical composition or the image of a work of art.

Sometimes one alternate personality may seem, both to the main personality and to an outside observer, to be knowledgeable and wise and beneficent, far beyond the capabilities and usual character of the host personality. Such an entity may claim to be a spirit guide, for instance. This is not dissimilar from the phenomenon of "channeling". The term channeling is usually used to connote a kind of communication which is external to the individual's "ordinary" conscious-unconscious mind system, and may seem in some respects to be quite superior to the ordinary mind. This "other" source may seem or claim to have been a person once alive on this Earth, or a being of some extraterrestrial sort not embodied in the usual physical sense. Other terms have been used for some forms of this phenomenon, at other times or under specific circumstances—these include "inspiration", "creativity", "deep intuition", "mediumship", "religious experience", and "revelation".

The history of science, mathematics, art, and intellectual achievement is replete with anecdotal episodes of this sort of communication seeming to come from somewhere other than the usual self. The revealed scriptures in many religious traditions are purported to have derived from such a source. Clearly the channeling experience, however interpreted, has profoundly affected the history of the human race. Yet science has had very little to say about the phenomenon, beyond admitting that most of its own conceptual advances seem to have arrived in this way. When something like this has been studied at all, it has been—like the studies of multiple personality—in the context of pathology.

As such research is pursued (as we can assume it will be, now that its potential importance has been widely recognized), it confronts us with a methodological question even more fundamental than those already raised. As deeper understanding of our own consciousness is sought, do we eventually encounter some questions that are indeed beyond science, beyond even some future extended form of science—although *not necessarily beyond ultimate human understanding*?

Suppose, for instance, that we were to conclude that in some cases of alternate personality, or channeling, there is contacted a source which appears to far exceed ordinary humans in intelligence, knowledge, and wisdom. Our tendency to ask of everything what it can be "used for" may in this case have to be curbed, for attempting to exploit such a source would be like the rat in the laboratory presuming to perform an experiment on the scientist. Our exuberant Western attitude that all of nature is here to be exploited for our ends may have to be replaced by a far more humble stance if we are to learn from the universe what it would teach us.

Creativity and Unconscious Knowing

It was mentioned earlier how we "know" in the unconscious mind much that is not ordinarily accessible to the conscious mind. This unconscious "knowing" is a far more pervasive aspect of experience than is ordinarily taken into account.

For example, research in biofeedback training discloses that we "know" unconsciously how to relax muscle tensions, change brain waves, alter heartbeat or blood pressure, change blood flow and skin temperature—but we aren't aware of this knowing until the feedback signal is provided. If I tape a small thermometer to read the temperature of the tip of my index finger, and focus my mind on how nice it would be if the temperature would rise five degrees, the temperature goes up! Unconsciously I know how to dilate the capillaries, increase the blood flow, and warm up the fingertip. Consciously I have no idea how to do this. I didn't know I knew, until provided with the feedback signal of the thermometer reading. Furthermore, once I get the "feel" of it I can dispense with the thermometer and warm the fingertip without it. (Children can do this with more facility than adults. It is not unusual for a young child, told to imagine the skin temperature very hot, to be able to raise it to 6 or 8 degrees above normal blood temperature!)

Unconsciously we "know" how to operate this remarkable organism called the physical body. We know how to produce peptic ulcers or alleviate them; to produce migraine headaches or be relieved of the pain; to heal wounds and restore damaged tissue, stopping with the appropriate quantity. We apparently know how to protect the soles of the feet so that they are unharmed while treading over burning coals. Unconsciously the pregnant woman knows how to create the fetus and initiate the birth process.

With our unconscious minds we know how to carry on mental activity that we can't do or even understand with the conscious mind. An everyday example is recalling information stored in the memory—for instance, somebody's name. Straining at it doesn't help: Let's see, now, does it begin with a P or a

B? Giving up for the moment, you "file a request" with another part of the mind to come up with the name. Sometime later, in the middle of a conversation on an unrelated topic, up pops the name! Unconsciously we know exactly how to search the memory files, identify the correct name from very scant clues, and bring the desired name up to conscious awareness. Consciously, we haven't the faintest idea how to accomplish this feat.

This may seem a very elementary example of what, when the task is more complex than memory, we call the creative process. The essence of creative problem-solving and intuitive decision guidance is much as it appears in this memory example. Creativity and intuition are terms we use to refer to those occasions when unconscious knowing is made accessible to the conscious mind. (So also are aesthetic experience and spiritual experience.) Sometimes there is a "request filed" for solution of a specific problem or answer to a question; sometimes the creative product simply arrives unbidden. But there is a part of the unconscious—a creative/intuitive mind—that knows how to find the solution or to produce the created product. And the key to creativity lies in opening up access to that mind, removing barriers, dissolving resistance.

In this drama of inner creativity there are at least three actors: the conscious mind, which wants to know; the creative/intuitive mind which knows; and yet another part of the unconscious which, for whatever reason, chooses to block or partially block access. (Not very long ago it would have been considered scientifically naive to speak in this way, but the experience of the fragmented mind with different parts "choosing" contradictory goals is one often described in contemporary literature on creativity.) One of the most powerful techniques for dissolving the resistance and releasing the creative abilities is that of affirmation (expression of self-fulfilling beliefs) and inner imagery.

Affirmation and Inner Imagery

Reprogramming the unconscious beliefs that block fuller awareness of our creative/intuitive capabilities depends upon a key characteristic of the unconscious mind, namely *that it responds to what is vividly imagined essentially as though it were real experience.* Thus, to revise the unconscious beliefs we need only vividly imagine new beliefs, and they tend to become "true". Because the unconscious beliefs have been reexperienced or reaffirmed repeatedly over a long period of time, the substitute beliefs and/or images must also be presented repetitiously over a period of time, preferably in a state of deep relaxation when the portals of the unconscious are most open. This basic principle is embodied in a variety of seminars and workshops and teaching techniques aimed at increasing effectiveness and releasing intuition and creativity.

There are many practical applications of the principle that what we affirm and program into the unconscious belief system, we tend in subtle ways to bring about. When we establish and affirm an intention or a goal, imagining that it is already so, the unconscious mind is programmed to achieve that goal even in ways which the conscious part of the mind does not plan or understand. Athletic coaches, for instance, train athletes to image championship performance. Doctors train cancer patients to heal themselves by imagining the functioning of the immune system in ridding the body of the cancer cells. Business executives learn to affirm that desired goals are already achieved. The basic principle has long been a core idea in the esoteric inner-core understandings of the world's spiritual traditions. The most familiar formulation in the Christian tradition is found in Mark 11:24—"Whatever you ask in prayer, believe that you receive it and you will."

In practice, the process of changing the unconsciously held beliefs may not seem as simple as just represented. As earlier noted, we tend to manifest resistance when presented with information or experience that would threaten the unconscious belief system. A hypnotized person will present fantastic rationalizations to deny evidence that conflicts with the picture he has agreed to perceive, or to explain why behavior directed by a post-hypnotic suggestion (that is, behavior in response to a suggestion from the hypnotist which the subject does not remember, cued by a signal of which the subject is unaware) is really perfectly reasonable behavior. The phenomenon of denial is familiar in psychotherapy; the client will actually fail to see what is apparent to any onlooker, because to see it would be too threatening.

Psychologist Abraham Maslow wrote eloquently about this matter in a chapter in *Toward a Psychology of Being* entitled "On the need to know and the fear of knowing". He observed that we are all ambivalent when it comes to knowing ourselves. We may consciously intend to use affirmations to reprogram the unconscious, and then because of the inner resistance we "forget" to carry out the exercises. We want to know where we are deceiving ourselves, but at the same time we will go to great lengths to avoid finding out. We have been thoroughly taught in Western culture not to trust ourselves—not to trust that ultimately we *do* know what we most deeply desire, and how to resolve our inner conflicts. We have been taught that beneath the thin veneer of the socialized conscious mind lurk who-knows-what animal urges, repressed hostilities, and other evils. We have been taught not to risk exploring the unconscious mind—at least not without a psychiatrist seated alongside in case we should get into trouble. And so we fear to know the fearsome and unsavory about ourselves. But as Maslow points out, "We find another kind of resistance, a denying of our best side, of our talents, of our finest impulse, of our highest potentialities, of our creativeness. . . . It is precisely the god-like in ourselves that we are ambivalent about, fascinated by and fearful of, motivated to and defensive against."

The Limits of Creativity

What then are the limits of the creative/intuitive mind? What is possible? We have already implied that the experienced limits are a function of the person's unconscious beliefs. If there is no reason in one's personal belief system to expect extraordinary performance from the creative unconscious mind, that assumption may limit the performance observed. Or inverting this observation, it is the oft-repeated testimony of successful executives and other creative people that the more one uses the creative/intuitive mind, the more faith one displays in turning to it with difficult decisions and problems, the better it seems to perform. And yet most people, dimly aware of its potentialities, deal with it as though it were marked FOR EMERGENCY USE ONLY. Even much of the literature on creativity encourages us in this—for instance, the assertion is often made in literature on creativity that one must strain to try to solve the problem with the conscious mind first, and absorb a great deal of information about the problem, before the behind-the-scenes creative mind will go to work. It is felt to be somehow cheating if one doesn't struggle first to solve the problem with the rational analytical mind, and only in desperation turn to the unconscious servant. Thus those who presumably teach the "techniques" of creativity are in many cases unwittingly teaching *limitations* as well.

Now comes a key question. If indeed one comes to learn that a liberated creative/intuitive mind can outperform the conscious rational mind (at least in some ways), why not turn over to it *all* questions and problems? Resistance to this idea is likely to be immediate and violent. For to assent to removing the ego-mind from its position of gatekeeper, governing what questions get asked of the creative unconscious, is to threaten its domination. To assent to accepting answers coming from the deep intuition is to assent to *not* guiding decisions by other means—plans, goals, ambitions, logical analyses, ethical rules, etc.—all the ways in which the rational ego-mind maintains its control (and all the ways we were taught in school as the right way to think). Yet this idea of submission to the deep intuition appears to be exactly what many successful persons in a wide variety of fields have come to adopt.

So what are the ultimate limits to creativity? The answer is not known, but we get some clues from a concept we will call the "spectrum of creativity". Near the "low" end of the creativity spectrum are all those accomplishments of the unconscious mind which strike us as mundane and familiar, hardly deserving of the term—maneuvering the car down the freeway while the conscious mind is otherwise occupied, as an example. Farther along are the more recognized phenomena of creative problem solving, intuitive judgment and hunches, aesthetic creation, etc. Some of these instances of creativity and creative problem solving are quite remarkable—as when a composer "hears" an entire musical composition in his "inner ear" and has only to copy it down, or an inventor intuits a complex solution to a problem. Still further toward the "high" end of the spectrum are instances of "automatic writing", in which the manuscript seems to pass directly from unconscious mind to writing hand without passing through the conscious mind. Other more extreme examples of creativity seem to involve the person having information not available by ordinary means (such as diagnosis of illness at a distance without seeing or knowing the patient) or even producing effects not possible by our usual understandings of reality (for example, abnormally rapid healing). Way out at the "high" end we might think of the more unbelievable miracles, and of the "grand inspirations" of the scriptures of some of the "divinely inspired" religious traditions.

Each person has some familiarity with phenomena along this spectrum. Each draws a line somewhere and insists that beyond that point the reported phenomena are incredible. Different people, and different societies, place the credibility marker at different points on the spectrum.

What is being discovered in research on human consciousness is that the perceptual bias of Western industrial society (which includes its predilection for objective, reductionistic science) has been limiting in a way that until recently was largely unsuspected. The more fully the spectrum of creativity is explored, the more it appears that the demarcation line between "plausible" and "preposterous" is largely a marker of our own resistance. Perhaps it does not perform a useful function at all. That does not mean, of course, that we should believe everything we see or hear. But it does mean that we need not cling so tenaciously to our beliefs that certain things shouldn't happen. As the Danish philosopher Soren Kierkegaard once remarked, there are two ways to be fooled: One is to believe what isn't so; the other is to refuse to believe what is so.

Again it is helpful to view this situation from the vantage points of the three metaphysics defined earlier. From the M-1 standpoint, science may someday be able to explain "ordinary creativity" in terms of something like rapid computer manipulations together with some sort of sensing device that can identify the right answer when the brain-computer cycles around to it. But for much of what lies out toward the "higher" end of the creativity spectrum this explanation seems very dubious indeed, and in fact it takes some straining to accommodate the concept of a "sensing device".

Viewed in M-2 or M-3, the situation can be accommodated with less strain. While creativity and intuition remain mysterious, there is at any rate no temptation to distort experience to fit preconceived limitations. And in the M-3 view in particular, *it is not clear that there are any limits to the human mind other than those we believe in.*

The "Perennial Wisdom" in Religion

We have spoken earlier of the power of affirmation and inner imagery as taught in seminars and workshops that have been increasingly accepted by the business world as valuable for executive development. Although the techniques vary somewhat from case to case, in essence the principle is simple and straightforward. The person is taught to imagine success, create a vision, in whatever form may be meaningful to that person—and hence to bring about success. The imagining is to be done in a disciplined way, a number of times a day, every day for weeks or months. In this process, which is closely related to autohypnosis, it helps to be in a state of deep relaxation when the achievement of the goal is affirmed or imaged.

Much of the seminar is devoted to persuading the person to believe enough to give the process a fair trial. The individual is encouraged to not assume any limits to what kind of a goal can be achieved, or how. Limits there may be, but when you believe in limits you may make them real—whether or not they might be otherwise.

Applying the principle that the deep intuition is our best judge of what goal to select, some of these executive development workshops go a step farther. They encourage an interplay between two states or activities. One is affirming the desired goal and expecting its achievement to come about. The other is referring to the deeper mind to find out what one *really* wants.

The two can in fact be combined in a single affirmation

something like the following: *I have no other desire than to know the deepest part of my Self, and to follow that.* I assume that what the deepest part of myself wants is what "I" want. I affirm that I have no other goals, ambitions, plans, and the like (that is, all the things I was taught to employ to "get ahead in life"), because those can be only concoctions of the ego-mind that deflect from what I really want.

There are two things to be noted here. One is that, as earlier noted, the business world is eminently practical. If this approach is used, it is because it works. It gets results. Never mind whether there is a theory to back it up; that can come later. The second observation is that there is a relationship between this key to effective living and age-old wisdom. Both parts of this approach are actually esoteric "secrets" that have been known for thousands of years, and are found in all the major spiritual traditions on the Earth.

These secrets were esoteric, or hidden, not because there was some inherent reason they had to be concealed from view, but because they tended to be antithetical or heretical to most societal belief systems. That is, to be known to practice them could be hazardous to your health (like being burned at the stake or tortured with one of those ingenious devices invented for carrying out the Inquisition). To put it another way: If you have discovered that it works out well to live your life based on an M-3 metaphysical assumption, but you happen to live in a rigidly authoritarian M-1 or M-2 society, be careful how you talk about your discovery!

We have already noted that the first part of this esoteric wisdom is expressed in Christian tradition in the proposition: "Whatever you pray for, believe that you receive it and you will". The second is also expressed in the form of prayer—not my will, but "Thy will be done". That certainly suggests that there is a relationship to religion to be explored.

One of the most important understandings of the last half century is of the conditions for a meaningful and effective life. This has arisen partly out of the experiences of psychotherapy and partly out of research in comparative religion. As the art of psychotherapy became increasingly free from its initial emphasis on pathology, and shifted more to helping well persons discover how to function even more effectively, the discovery of untapped inner resources became a central focus. William James' *Varieties of Religious Experience* had long ago argued that the central core of religious experience appeared to be that the person identifies his real being with "the germinal higher part of himself" and then "becomes conscious that this higher part is co-terminous and continuous with a MORE of like quality, which is operative in the universe outside of him, and which he can keep in working touch with, and in a fashion get on board of and save himself when all his lower being has gone to pieces in the wreck". Transpersonal psychotherapy had uncovered a similar principle.

Meanwhile in the field of comparative religion a profound and related discovery had been made. Aldous Huxley was the first to announce it in a popular book, freed of weighty technical jargon, in 1945—in *The Perennial Philosophy*. It was this: When the various religions of the world and of history are studied, it is found they each fall into two types. First, each religion has one or more *exoteric* or public forms. These are what we usually think of when the term religion is used. They are characterized by their rituals, the architecture of their halls of worship, their revealed literature, and so on. But besides this, each spiritual tradition tends to have an *esoteric* or secret version, known only to an inner circle, and usually involving some sort of meditative discipline. The range of exoteric religions is fantastically diverse. However, all of the esoteric traditions are essentially the same—or, more precisely, appear to be based in some form of potentially universal spiritual experience. This common core has sometimes been referred to as the "perennial wisdom".

This esoteric "perennial wisdom" of the world's spiritual traditions is not a theory or a hypothesis to be articulated in ways familiar in scientific and philosophical treatises. Aldous Huxley says of it: "Nothing in our everyday experience gives us much reason for supposing that the mind of the average sensual man has, as one of its constitutents, something resembling, or identical with, the Reality substantial to the manifold world; and yet, when that mind is subjected to certain rather drastic treatments, the divine element, of which it is at least in part composed, becomes manifest, not only to the mind itself, but also, by its reflection in external behaviour, to other minds. . . . It is only by making psychological and moral experiments that we can discover the intimate nature of mind and its potentialities. In the ordinary circumstances of average sensual life these potentialities of the mind remain latent and unmanifested. If we would realize them, we must fulfill certain conditions and obey certain rules, which experience has shown empirically to be valid." Among the "rather drastic treatments" Huxley refers to may be included various forms of yoga, meditative disciplines, ascetic vision quests, and shamanic rituals.

This "perennial wisdom", being a distillation of the experience of many inner explorers over thousands of years, is without doubt an invaluable guide. It is also in principle compatible with any of the religious traditions since it is found in all of them; the long-standing conflict between the exoteric and the esoteric seems to have lost some of its hold. Although it may not have seemed so in the past, the "perennial wisdom" is also in principle compatible with science.

Science and the "Perennial Wisdom"

The modern world long assumed that there was a fundamental incompatibility between science and religion. For a time it appeared as a series of direct conflicts over such issues as the age of the Earth, the meaning of the fossil records, evolutionary theory, the Freudian re-interpretation of the human soul and so forth. Religion always seemed to lose. Then as the world moved well into the twentieth century the conflict subsided, and people tended to live their religious lives apart from whatever they thought science was telling them about the nature of reality. The price paid for this schizophrenia was that neither science nor religion fully satisfied the person's desire to *know* with inner certainty. But now it becomes apparent that whereas there may indeed be conflict between positivistic science and dogmatic, exoteric religion, there is no necessary conflict at all between the esoteric "perennial wisdom" and a science based on an M-3 metaphysic.

We can try to make this a little more specific by considering some aspects of the "perennial wisdom" and indicating how science is already approaching them. But let us not be misunderstood. Science has not, is nowhere near, and presumably never will "prove" the inner understanding we are referring to by the term "perennial wisdom". The "perennial wisdom", in turn, is not, and presumably never will be, articulated in a form such that it can be tested in a scientific manner. It may be, however, exemplified in a life, and "proved" by living it. The best scientific knowledge available would seem at the least not to contradict it, and at most to tend to support it.

The French poet St. Exupery said, "Truth is not that which is demonstrable. Truth is that which is ineluctable"—which cannot be escaped. Science deals with the demonstrable. The "perennial wisdom" insists that the ineluctable is found only through exploration of, and identification with, the deep Self.

We can point, in a general way, to this relationship between science and the "perennial wisdom" by considering six headings:

Consciousness. Of all the findings of modern psychology, one of the most firmly established, and the one with the most pervasive implications, is that only a small part of our total mental activity is conscious. The more vast portion is out of conscious awareness—in the unconscious. Ordinary conscious awareness may be thought of as a narrow "visible spectrum" between the subconscious (for example, instinctual drives, repressed memories, autonomic functioning) and the supraconscious (for example, creative imagination, intuitive judgment, aesthetic sense, spiritual sensibility).

Some of this out-of-consciousness activity is, so to speak, in the "deep unconscious" and we become aware of it only through inference. Some of it is at least partly accessible to conscious awareness under certain conditions (such as through hypnotic suggestion, dreaming, biofeedback training, meditation, autogenic training). Access to unconscious processes is facilitated by attention to feelings, emotions, and inner imagery.

All of the above is compatible with the "perennial wisdom", but that tradition goes farther. It finds that there is a creative/intuitive/spiritual mind which is not limited in ways we might expect the mind to be limited. Access to it, and indeed identification with this deep Center, can be facilitated by various meditative disciplines, again to an extent that is ultimately unlimited. Man's deepest ecological, humane, moral, and spiritual commitments are all rooted in this realm of human experience.   As Ralph Waldo Emerson put it, when this other mind "breathes through his intellect, it is genius; when it breathes through his will, it is virtue; when it flows through his affection, it is love. And the blindness of the intellect begins when it would be something of itself."

Perception. Perception is greatly affected by unconscious beliefs, which in turn are shaped by suggestion, expectation, influence of authority, cultural beliefs, etc.   This conclusion is supported by extensive and varied clinical and experimental research and anthropological studies.   Seeing may be believing, but what is seen is not necessarily what is there. (One of the more startling examples of altered perception is when, through hypnotic suggestion, a person is led to perceive what isn't there.) In fact, when the influence of unconscious conditioning on perception is fully taken into account, the more accurate statement might be "Believing is seeing".

Here again the "perennial wisdom", while compatible with contemporary science, goes farther. We are literally hypnotized from infancy by the cultural milieu in which we are immersed; we see the world the way we are enculturated to see it. A prime task of adult life is to become dehypnotized, "enlightened"—to see reality as it is and to "know thy Self". In this process we come to realize that we, in the out-of-consciousness collective mind, create the world of ordinary experience—which we then experience with the conscious mind.

Oneness. Whether or not one chooses to think in terms of "extrasensory communication", there is a kind of experience known to everyone in which individual consciousness communicates at a deep level with the consciousness of others. We refer to this experience with words like "rapport" and "love".

Research on telepathic communication, while not totally convincing to the skeptical, reinforces the impression that we sometimes know what is going on in other minds, without any of the usual physical sensory cues. In fact that knowledge may not be accessible to conscious awareness. (In one such experiment a flashing strobe light stimulus in one person's eyes produces an electrical component in the EEG pattern of another, distant and isolated, who has no physical indication of and no conscious awareness of the remote strobe light's flashing.)

In the "perennial wisdom", this awareness of rapport and of being joined is referred to in yet another sense. In higher states of consciousness there is an awareness of being one with the universe and all its creatures, of a knowing—a *gnosis*—related to that of the Creator. Because these kinds of insights are so different from the ordinary experience our language usually expresses, they are not easily conceptualized and verbally communicated. Myth and symbol, paradox, poetic metaphor become more effective means of communicating these insights and experiences.

Resistance. We humans are well known to be ambivalent with respect to our desire to know ourselves. We will resist that knowledge which we most deeply desire.

We think we want to see reality as it is, to see truthfully. But our illusions are part of an unconsciously held belief system; any attack on those illusions is perceived (unconsciously) as a threat. Thus an effort to dispel illusion, though ultimately beneficial, may nevertheless generate resistance. We truly desire to discover and actualize our highest intuitive capacities, yet to the extent that removing illusion is essential to that discovery, we will resist that which we truly desire. (We may, in fact, resist it by using the most convincing "scientific" arguments and concepts.)

The ego self is threatened by the existence of the real Self and throws up a variety of smokescreens to block awareness of the true Center. In the end, for integration the ego self must become subservient to the real Self.

Creativity. The creative/intuitive capacities operate outside of conscious awareness in solving problems and providing answers to posed questions. Limits to the creative/intuitive mind arise from unconscious beliefs (such as "I am inadequate and unworthy"; "failure and ridicule are to be feared"). In general, its performance can be enhanced by intention, expectation, trust, and belief in the efficacy of the deep mind.

Trust in the creative/intuitive mind implies nonattachment to the goals of the rational/analytical mind.

The mystery of the creative/intuitive mind is underscored in the "perennial wisdom", which finds the deep intuition connected to the one Universal Mind. Thus there are indeed no limits to its capabilities save those the individual creates as part of the resistance to discovering one's godlike qualities. Furthermore, because of this connection to the All, problem solutions which come from the deep intuition will be solutions that benefit all, not one at the expense of others.

Choice. Each of us, as we naturally stand, is fragmented. We make choices at unconscious as well as conscious levels, and they are not necessarily in alignment. Viewed in this light, the psychodynamic defense mechanisms can be thought of as unconscious choices. Repression is a choice to hide information from oneself; denial and resistance are choices not to perceive that which would imply change. Choices effected by the "authoritarian conscience", the introjected parent, Freud's superego, are likewise unconscious choices. On the other hand, choice may be guided by the supraconscious intuitive, aesthetic, or spiritual sense. Values are guides for choice which have been integrated into the personality or cultural pattern; in general, they have an unconscious component.

To anyone who is still at some stage of resistance to recognizing his/her inner abilities, the "perennial wisdom" appears to make an extreme, even startling leap when it comes to the matter of choice-guidance. When the other stages of awakening the inner senses are fully realized, the esoteric teachings enjoin us to turn over *all* choices to the deep intuition, the "authentic conscience". Only in this way does the person become totally integrated (a person of integrity), with the whole of one's being—subconscious, conscious, and supraconscious—directed toward the same ends. This fundamental decision implies having no other ambitions, seeking no other goals. Hence the admonition—"abandon all to have all".

These observations are not a demonstration of an incontrovertible conclusion. They do not argue that science will end up "proving" the "perennial wisdom".

Science does seem to be in the process of further substantiating that most of our mental activity is out of conscious awareness; that our "unconscious knowing" goes much farther than we might have imagined; and that our "unconscious choosing" has both tyrannical and liberating aspects. These findings are at least compatible with, and perhaps extrapolate to, the "perennial wisdom". That suggests that in the end science and religion are not at odds, but are complementary ways of knowing—both being essential to achieving the highest measure of what it means to be human.

Toward a More Comprehensive Science

As we have seen, modern science adopted, at an early stage in its history, the stance of objectivism, positivism, and reductionism. For practical and political reasons that were quite valid at the time, the scientific enterprise became characterized by three assumptions which have become almost synonymous with "scientific method":

- The *objectivist* assumption, that there is an objective universe which can be explored by the methods of scientific inquiry, and which can be approximated, progressively more precisely, by quantitative models;
- The *positivist* assumption, that what is scientifically "real" must take as its basic data only that which is physically observable; and
- The *reductionist* assumption, that scientific explanation consists in explaining complex phenomena in terms of more elemental events (for example, gas temperature and pressure in terms of the motions of the molecules; human behavior in terms of stimulus and response).

These characteristics have seemed so integral to the scientific method that it is hard to imagine they would ever be displaced. Yet the data of exceptional abilities and the "inner empiricism" of the esoteric spiritual traditions challenge them in a way that may bring about a major revolutionary advance.

Science has a long history of defending the bulwarks against the persistent reports of phenomena and experiences that "don't fit in"—such as the spiritual and religious, the exceptionally creative and intuitive, the "miraculous" in healing and regeneration, the paranormal, seemingly teleologically motivated instinctual patterns, etc. But these defensive efforts have often seemed to be unfruitful and divisive.

One wonders if we have not become trapped in the quagmire of our own dogmas. Is there not a way to escape from these dilemmas without sacrificing any of the intellectual rigor, open spirit of inquiry, and public validation of knowledge that characterize science at its best?

Suppose, instead of the stance adopted because of history and circumstance, science were to adopt a different approach, namely, to *assume the validity of any type of human experience or extraordinary ability which is consistently reported down through the ages, or across cultures, and adapt science in such a way as to accommodate all of these.* Let us explore some of the characteristics of such an extended science.

Holistic models and hierarchical causes. In contrast with conventional science, such a more comprehensive science will include more emphasis on holistic models and will center around some concept of hierarchically related causes. Let us illustrate this with some simple examples.

It may seem almost obvious that *the whole is qualitatively different from the sum of the parts.* A chemical compound displays qualities quite different from the qualities of any of its separate ingredients. An ecological system has characteristics one would not have suspected from simply examining its component organisms. A culture has characteristics that are not simply the sum of the behaviors of the individuals who compose it. The human body is not simply the sum of its organs and tissues.

Yet that basic principle has implications with regard to causative models which have not been appreciated through the history of science; that lack of appreciation has led to bitter dissents. *If characteristics emerge at higher system levels that are qualitatively different from those at lower levels, then the sciences ap-*

propriate to different system levels will be qualitatively different. The science of cells is qualitatively different from the science of organisms, which in turn differs from the science of ecological systems.

A simple extension of this principle leads to the concept of a hierarchy of complementary and mutually non-contradictory "explanations" for the same phenomenon. The factors that enter into an explanation at one level of system complexity may be meaningless at another level. Thus at one level of system hierarchy a conscious decision to act may be part of the explanation, whereas at another level we can comprehend only non-volitional, physical forces.

For example, suppose that I come down with a cold. At one level of explanation we may say that a virus "causes" the cold. But viruses, bacteria and a vast assortment of other microorganisms inhabit the space known as "my body" all the time. Some are beneficial, such as the bacteria in the intestines that are so essential to the digestive process. If we include in this accounting the body cells, I am "really" a vast ecological community of microorganisms which exist in a state of largely cooperative balance—most of the time. If this ecology gets out of balance, perhaps following my taking a chill, then I am said to have a particular disease, characterized by that imbalance. Put another way, the body's immune system functioning—which, after all, is the consequence of actions of a host of "friendly" microorganisms, T-cells and the like—is impaired, and that is why I have the cold. That is another level of explanation.

At yet another explanatory level we may observe that the reason the ecology of bodily microorganisms got out of balance was something called "stress". Stress is a psychological response to the environment such that various glandular secretions increase, and the body gets ready for "fight or flight". Repeated or continuous stress in situations where fleeing is unseemly and physical fighting is impermissible can lead to malfunction of the immune system—hence susceptibility to colds.

These three explanations, each valid in its own way, are at different levels in some sort of hierarchy. Moving from the first to the second to the third, there is a progressive increase in the amount of the universe included in the system under consideration. Furthermore, the causal agents are different at the different levels. At one level it may be the cold virus; at another, the condition of the body's immune system; at another, attitudes toward home and work which bring on the stress condition. These causal agents are progressively less physical and more abstract. Note that the abstract causes are not less "scientific" than the others; they merely occur at different levels in the hierarchy.

At a less sophisticated stage of science there was a tendency to consider the level of physical causation to be somehow more "real" than the more abstract levels (positivism). Thus for example there was considerable initial resistance to the idea of psychosomatic illness, or to the idea that positive emotions might have a salutary effect on the body's immune system. Furthermore, "scientific explanation" tended to imply interpretation at the level of physical causation (reductionism). Thus teleological causes (explanations involving purpose) were ruled out. A reaction of the arm to an external stimulus could be dealt with scientifically, but an arm movement *for the purpose of reaching a desired object* could not. The need is increasingly apparent to somehow extend science beyond the restrictions of this predilection for the physical level.

The hierarchical structuring of science. Let us consider one such schema for structuring scientific knowledge in a hierarchical way—not a new concept in the philosophy of science (see Popper, 1977), but one that has never been really taken seriously by mainstream scientists.

Imagine a set of bookshelves, the shelves of which are labeled, upward from the bottom shelf: "Physical Sciences", "Life Sciences", "Human Sciences", and "Spiritual Sciences". The volumes on the "Physical Sciences" shelves deal with the physical sciences, more or less in their present form. In the volumes on the "Life Sciences" shelf we find expositions of the biological and health sciences. Here, however, we encounter holistic concepts like "organism", and teleological concepts like "function", that are foreign to the discussions on the bottom shelf. Discussions of the "Human Sciences" on the third shelf contain even more holistic and abstract concepts like "personal health" and "personality" and "individual purpose". The fourth shelf labeled "Spiritual Sciences" (required if the deep subjective experience of untold mystics, prophets, artists, and poets, down through the ages, is to be honored) deals with the suprapersonal. Here we find discussed still more abstract concepts, perhaps, such as "universal purpose". (The diagram hints at how the topics of health care and evolution might involve qualitatively different concepts when approached from the four levels.)

Four Levels of Models and Explanations

Level	Health example	Evolution example
4. Spiritual sciences	Spiritual health; wholeness	Universal purpose
3. Human sciences	Individual biological health	Individual purpose
2. Life sciences	Organ function; illness	System function; natural selection
1. Physical sciences	Metabolism rate; body temperature	Molecular biology; mutation; physical characteristics

It is apparent that an extensive "level-1" science of the physical world already exists. In the life sciences and psychiatric theory there are fragments of a "level-2" science which repudiates the claims of some molecular biologists that eventually all behavior is explained by the genes. As for "level-3" science, humanistic psychology and sociology are even more fragmentary. At the fourth level we find attempts such as transpersonal psychology and Tibetan Buddhist psychology.

Behavioral conditioning may seem to fit comfortably at level 2, whereas volition, intention, comprehension, and paying attention are level-3 concepts; values and meaning may be thought of in terms of level-4 concepts. James Lovelock's "Gaia hypothesis" considers the Earth as a self-regulating organism; in its most widely accepted form it is a level-2 concept, but some would attribute consciousness to the planet a level-4 hypothesis.

In systematic biology, a level-2 science, the quality of connoisseurship becomes important in species recognition. Empathy may be a desirable characteristic of the scientist at level 3. At level 4 one encounters the problem of a limited number of qualified observers (qualified in terms of their own inner development), and it has been extremely difficult to avoid the pitfalls of dogma and cult.

Further characteristics of a hierarchically structured science. We need to note a number of further characteristics of such a hierarchically extended science.

Questions asked. Questions not appropriate at one level of models *may nevertheless fit at another.* Thus teleological questions have no place in the level of reductionistic science of physical reality. At the next level, however, it is appropriate to ask about the function of the body's immune system, or of elaborate instinctive patterns in animal behavior. At the third level volition may be acceptable as a causal factor, and personality is a meaningful construct; one can inquire into the significance of personal acts and habit patterns. At the suprapersonal or spiritual level questions about "other kinds of consciousness" achieved in meditative states, and guidance of choices by some kind of deep intuition, may be meaningful.

In the past, scientists have tended to insist that teleological questions and value-focused questions are not appropriate to science. Of course, they have always been asked in some areas, such as the health sciences. A question about the function of some part of the body's regulatory system is teleological, and certainly a question about what leads toward health is value-focused.

To those who still ask whether these kinds of questions are

appropriate to science, one can reply with the question, "If not science, then what?" There is no other authority in modern society with the prestige of science to ask these important questions.

Models and metaphors. The models and metaphors used at one explanatory level may be obviously inappropriate at another. The holistic metaphors appropriate to considering human personality are "nonphysical" and do not appear at the physical level; on the other hand, atomistic explanations of organic processes at the physical level leave out the essence of what is being studied at the higher levels.

It should be noted that there need be no claim to exclusivity in terms of which level is ultimately "real". Physicists led the way in the recognition that reality is too rich to be fully expressed in any model, theory, metaphor, or equation. Wave models do not invalidate particle models, and vice-versa; the two metaphors are *complementary*, not contradictory. Similarly, an explanation of human behavior in terms of the philosophy of life adopted does not contradict, but rather complements, an explanation in terms of repressed desires and conditioned responses.

A scientist may behave professionally as though the physical level describes what is "real". Another scientist (or for that matter, the same one) may lead his/her personal life as though only the suprapersonal level of mind and spirit points to the ultimately real. There is no contradiction involved, and the individual does not become a schizoid personality for holding both views at the same time. Indeed, a person may be a better scientist for not having to fight so strongly to defend the positivism and reductionism appropriate to the physical level.

Of course there are aberrations to be avoided, arising from adopting too extreme a position. The extreme positivist, reductionist position leads to having to deny the reality of the most immediate experience, such as that of attention and volition. The extreme suprapersonal position can result in a person who is ineffective through not being "grounded".

Methodology. The methodology used is that appropriate to a given level and may be quite different for a different explanatory level. The rigidly controlled experiment, and the expectation of strict reliability of experimental results, are appropriate to the physical level and, to a more limited extent, the organismic. Even at these levels there may be intrusions of observer effect which are understandable from higher levels but "anomalous" at the lower.

The idea that the scientific observer can not be "objective" in the sense of isolating himself completely from the phenomena observed applies at all levels to some extent, and particularly at the higher ones. What the scientist perceives is a function of unconscious conditioning and previous suggestions picked up from the environment. Furthermore, as the universe is perceived from the higher levels, the contents and processes of the experimenter's mind can affect the experiment in ways not understandable from the lower explanatory levels.

These kinds of considerations become especially relevant whenever "consciousness as causal reality" is a significant factor in the phenomena being observed. They suggest that strict interpretations of objectivity and of reliability through replicability are inappropriate in research on subjective experience. That surely, if they are, there must be other criteria something like these which *are* appropriate. Perhaps as the scientific exploration of these areas becomes more mature, something like the Buddhist ideal of "nonattachment" will indeed replace the concept of strict objectivity which, as is well known, no longer seems to fit even the relatively dependable area of the physical sciences. And something like "trustworthiness" (perhaps established on the basis of multiple imperfect tests) may replace strict reliability through replicability.

Consider as an example the research on multiple personalities discussed earlier. Is it really true that, incredible as it may seem at first thought, the same body may be inhabited by more than one personality? This holistic concept can hardly be explored at all without interacting with the person(s); thus objectivity in any strict sense is inappropriate. However, the ideal of nonattachment to preconceived notions of what can and cannot be is clearly pertinent. Not too long ago, the concept of an alternative personality expressing itself through the same body depended almost entirely on the psychiatrist's impressions. The concept has gained credibility in recent years because of the discovery that when the personality shifts, various measures of bodily functioning also change (the striking example being a person who is allergic to something with one personality not being allergic with another!).

One other methodological point is important to note. In carrying out research that involves higher explanatory levels, the observer is not unchanged by his scientific activities. One cannot explore altered states of consciousness without being sensitized and otherwise changed in the process.

It is also the case that a willingness to be transformed is an essential characteristic of the scientist of the higher explanatory levels. The cultural anthropologist who would see clearly another culture than his own must allow that experience to change him so that the new culture is seen through new eyes, not eyes conditioned by the scientist's own culture. The psychotherapist who would see her client clearly must have worked through her own neuroses which would otherwise warp perception. The scientist who would study at the level we have called "spiritual science" has to be willing to go through the changes that will make him/her a competent observer.

Data admitted. It seems clear that the new science will in some way have to deal with subjective reports of deep inner experience. When this has been put forward in the past the idea was rejected by the main body of scientists. Perhaps it will come forward now in more sophisticated form.

At the level of "physical reality" admissible data is primarily in the form of quantifiable physical observation. At the organism level somewhat more holistic kinds of observations become important, such as instinctive behavior patterns, or the functioning of the digestive system. Self-reports of inner, subjective experience become relevant at the personal level, and essentially comprise the sole source of data at the suprapersonal level.

"Upward-looking" and "downward-looking" explanations. Reductionism has been so characteristic of most science that one almost automatically thinks of scientific explanation in those

terms. We understand (scientifically) a phenomenon when we can describe it in terms of more elemental phenomena. Prestige is given to an explanation of behavior of a living organism in terms of responses to external stimuli, biochemical tensions, DNA composition and structure, etc.—in other words, *downward-looking* explanation.

Complementary Modes of Explanation

Yet it is clear that scientists also use (often reluctantly) *upward-looking* explanation—explanation in terms of concepts at a higher level (Sperry, 1987). For example, when the immune system attacks a particular virus it is not understood as just a complex chemical reaction; it can only be really understood in terms of the *function* of the immune system being to protect the organism from harm (a level-2 concept). In regeneration of a lobster claw after amputation, the complex building process can only be understood in terms of some kind of morphogenetic image of the nature of a whole lobster claw. To understand altruistic behavior it is necessary to invoke at least level-3, and possibly level-4, concepts. Teleological explanation (in terms of purpose or goal) is only one form of upward-looking explanation.

It is as though in the diagram shown the physical-sciences shelf and the downward-looking arrow have been in boldface throughout most of the history of science. Only in very recent years are we ready to consider seriously the complete knowledge system implied by the rest of the diagram.

At the same time that we recognize the validity of both downward-looking and upward-looking explanations, we need to note that the basic hunger for meaning, for making sense out of our lives, which is so characteristic of the human condition, tends to be more satisfied by the upward-looking explanations. They may or may not be more fundamental by some rational argument, but they *feel* more fundamental.

The reframing of unfruitful controversy. One of the most important results of coming to think about science in this hierarchically structured way is that many of the scientific controversies of the past simply disappear when we reframe them in terms of such levels of explanations. The behaviorist issue is clearly a matter of a certain group of scientists insisting that they will not deal with what is not at the level of physical measurability. The perennial "free will versus determinism" debate is resolved simply by recognizing that these are two complementary concepts that fit on different levels. Dualistic approaches amount to considering only two levels, rather than at least four. Miraculous healings, such as those meeting the stringent criteria set by the International Medical Commission at Lourdes, France, may in the end be considered to fit at the suprapersonal level and to not contravene the usefulness of the physical and organismic levels of explanation for many other purposes. One of these perennial controversies has been over interpretation of the phenomena of *morphogenesis*. Morphogenesis (literally, the birth of form) is particularly evident in healing, regeneration (restoration of a mutilated organism), and embryonic growth. An extreme form of regeneration is found in some simple animals, like hydra or planaria, where a tiny fragment of the organism can regenerate a complete individual. In embryonic growth, multiplication of a single cell eventually results in the formation of a complete organism, with many diverse cells performing widely differentiated functions. In order to explain the phenomena, the concept has been introduced of a vital force, peculiar to living organisms, that directs form and development. "Vitalism", as this idea has been termed, has in general been very controversial in the scientific community. The term "morphogenetic field" has been used since the 1920s to describe the organizing principle whereby the many cells are guided to combine, with differentiated functions, to produce a living organism of particular form. (The same term was later extended by Rupert Sheldrake to account for complex instinctual behaviors in animals.) But there seems to be no satisfactory way of explaining morphogenesis at the physical level; some higher-level concept appears to be required.

A somewhat similar controversy is present with regard to evolution (complicated by the fact that fundamentalist Christianity and the US Supreme Court are also in the act). The prevailing neo-Darwinist theory tends to account for the evolution of high-order species through random mutation and natural selection. This, however, leaves many puzzles, not the least of which is that posed by structures (such as the two eyes for binocular vision) which would appear to have no survival value in any intermediate stage, so that it is hard to imagine their evolution taking place in any sort of incremental way—and equally hard to imagine through a sudden transformational leap. It seems possible that a more adequate theory of the evolutionary process will eventually include both the neo-Darwinist sort of mechanism and some higher-level morphogenetic directing force, something like a universal (or at least planetary) mind.

Not all such controversy is so easily removed. For example, astrology has been sustained for thousands of years by empirical generalizations based on the predictions of horoscopes; if there is ever to be a robust theory of astrological influence it will obviously have to be at a suprapersonal level. Again, the seventeenth-century destruction of belief in phenomena related to witchcraft, shamanism, animism, and the like, was in the face of overwhelming evidence supporting existence of the phenomena; new kinds of acceptable explanations may well appear in time, but they will have to be at a personal (for example as phenomena of hypnosis) or suprapersonal level.

Particular mention should be made of the principle of parsimony—the idea that a simpler and more aesthetically elegant conceptualization should be preferred to a more elaborate or complex one, when both accommodate the known facts. This principle would seem to have been often misapplied in the past, when it has been used to disallow explanations at the higher levels in favor of straining to reinterpret (or disallow) data to fit the explanation into the physical level.

Explanatory concepts at one level may be very useful in complementing the primary explanations of phenomena at some different level. The conceptualizations at the physical level, for example, may add rich detail to psychosomatic processes where the basic explanation appears to be at a higher level. The highly sophisticated suprapersonal conceptualizations of the Tibetan Buddhist psychologies, on the other hand, may contribute important insights into processes at the personal and organismic levels.

A Concluding Comment

The importance of the issues raised here can hardly be overestimated. It can be indicated by one simple observation. We in modern society give tremendous prestige and power to our official, publicly validated knowledge system, namely science. It is unique in this position; none of the coexisting knowledge systems—not any system of philosophy or theology, nor philosophy or theology as a whole—is in a comparable position. Thus it is critically important—to an unparalleled degree—that our science is adequate. *It is impossible to create a well-working society on a knowledge base which is fundamentally inadequate, seriously incomplete, and mistaken in basic assumptions.* Yet that is precisely what the modern world has been trying to do.

If one takes seriously the implication that Western science is an artifact of Western society, based on implicit assumptions compatible with that society's basic reality outlook, it follows that the primary impetus for a fundamental change in its underlying assumptions will come not from scientists, but from the surrounding culture. Indeed, we see much evidence over the past quarter century that such a force may be gathering. Thus the relevance of this critique is as much to the public at large as to the scientist. With this in mind, we have deliberately kept this argument simple, and minimized the amount of supportive detail and qualifications. The basic concept is a simple one, and can be understood by non-scientists. The cost of past dogma-versus-dogma conflicts, within and outside science, has been too high. We can no longer afford it. The remedy may be to promote something like the hierarchically arranged explanatory levels suggested above. It would certainly seem preferable to continued conflict over the evolution issue, the parapsychology issue, the vitalism issue, the holism/reductionism issue, the science-versus-religion issue, and so on ad infinitum.

Thus we end this chapter with a conclusion that has the most profound implications for all societies: There appears indeed to be no conflict between a mature science and a mature religion. Indeed, we must seriously question whether we have a mature science as long as such conflict appears to exist.

5

We stand on the brink of . . . a new age: the age of an open world and of a self capable of playing its part in that larger sphere . . . Every goal [humanity] . . . reaches provides a new starting point, and the sum of all [humanity's] . . . days is just a beginning.
                    —*Lewis Mumford*

Transforming
the
World Macroproblem

Why is this change in underlying metaphysic taking place now, in the last quarter of the twentieth century? Partly, no doubt, it is because science has become more mature. The recognition that science has had an intrinsic bias is not as threatening as it would have been a half century or more ago. It is much easier to accept that inner, subjective experience has been a neglected area which requires some new approach to handle it.

For one thing, the physicists have long since made it clear that science deals with *models* of reality; hence it is not so surprising to find that any given model does not adequately represent *all* aspects of reality. Niels Bohr's introduction of the concept of *complementarity* into quantum physics was an important step in this maturing process: Wave models and particle models of light turned out to be complementary rather than contradictory, in that each represented certain observable aspects of the mystery of light. So too might matter-energy models and mind-spirit-consciousness models turn out to express complementary aspects of the mystery of life.

Quantum physics has brought some additional surprises. From a "thought experiment" devised by three physicists and referred to as the "Einstein-Podolsky-Rosen paradox", later verified in the laboratory, it appears that if two particles have been intimately associated and are then separated in space, they are "connected" nonetheless. If one of them is perturbed in certain ways, the other one is affected *instantaneously*. (The connectedness, in other words, does not depend on a signal traveling at the speed of light or slower.)

Related to this experiment is a mathematical demonstration called Bell's theorem, which is essentially that everything in the universe is connected. More specifically, it falsifies the "principle of local causes", which holds that a phenomenon can be explained in terms of causes in the immediate space-time vicinity. That is, the results of an experiment conducted here and now would not be expected to be affected by what is happening at some spot in the universe remote in space or time or both. (For example, the images in my mind would not be expected to be affected by the fact that on the other side of the continent a loved one has just been involved in a serious automobile accident.) Bell's theorem denies this "commonsense" assumption. Physicist David Bohm theorizes more generally that we can never understand reality in terms of particles and fields alone; we must ultimately perceive the "unbroken wholeness" in a non-reductionistic way.

In sum, the ultimate triumph of reductionistic physics is to demonstrate the *necessity* of a new paradigm which goes beyond reductionistic science.

Other factors that are not directly related to developments in science are influencing the shift in paradigm as well. One of the most important of these is that with increased education and understanding, in the last half century the omnipresence of the "perennial wisdom" in the world's spiritual traditions has become apparent and widely accepted. (Before that most explorations of other religious traditions than Christianity and Judaism had been as anthropological or historical curiosities, not as records of human experience from which we might learn.) Not only has it now become clear that the "perennial wisdom" is compatible with all the world's spiritual traditions, since it is at the heart of each, but the supposed conflict with science is turning out to be not as real as had been earlier assumed.

In addition to these reasons, the contemporary reassessment of basic assumptions is also a consequence of the growing suspicion that without some sort of fundamental change, modern industrial society appears to be unable to resolve the sociopolitical and ecological dilemmas that beset us. Not only does each decade seem to be more problem-laden than the last, the problems seem more and more intertwined, and the tradeoffs get progressively less and less favorable. The change required is not simply a shift from one form of industrial society to another (such as capitalism to socialism), but rather a major change in the basic assumptions underlying both versions of industrial society.

To get a fresh perspective on this latter observation, let us perform a little thought experiment.

A Different Perspective

Imagine yourself to be an anthropologist from another civilization—let's say on another planet—visiting the Earth for the first time. You soon sense, especially as you talk with the children, that there is a lot of insecurity about the future. In particular, the brooding presence of tens of thousands of nuclear weapons already aimed at preselected cities and military targets forces awareness, at least at an unconscious level, that the world is ready to blow itself up. What is the reason for all that insecurity? you inquire. The answer: The quest for national *security!*

You note that the insecurity in vast regions of the world takes another form. World distribution of food, income, and wealth is extremely uneven—far more uneven than is the distribution in any single country, even those with the most notoriously unjust political orders. Yet there appears to be no workable proposal to correct this situation. Instead, economic and demographic forces seem inexorably to cause the maldistribution to grow steadily worse. The rich "North" partakes of a feast that the world's limited resources can sustain only with increasing difficulty, while the teeming populations of the impoverished "South" remain trapped in a remorseless cycle of deprivation that revolves around poverty, illiteracy, and high birthrates. The threat of ultimate "wars of redistribution" grows ever more imminent. Meanwhile the two superpowers squabble between themselves, each fearful of the intent of the other, holding the Earth's population hostage to their unprecedented capabilities to lay waste the entire planet.

You discover something else fundamentally strange about the structure of the most powerful societies on the planet—they place in paramount position, as guard of the most precious values of the society, *economic* institutions, rather than those institutions that have to do with wisdom, knowledge, learning, religion! You see no obvious reason to believe that economic logic and economic values will ever lead to wise social decisions. Curiouser and curiouser!

For example, you find that virtuous behavior is defined by the leading institutions to be economic consumption, so much so that citizens, especially in the United States of America, refer to one another as fellow "consumers". Frugality, once a central virtue, is subtly discouraged as being bad for the economy!

Why is so much consumption required? you inquire. To use up the production, you are informed. (The global arms race is good for that, too.) The economic indicators, such as the GNP, which measure how well the society is doing, are essentially measures of how rapidly resources are being used up—converted to economic product. The more economic product, the "healthier" the economy and, by implication, the society.

Is that good, you ask, on a finite planet to place a premium on the maximum rate of using up resources? It is necessary in order to create jobs, you hear in response, and to create purchasing power so that there will be a market for all that economic product. You reflect again on that historical document *Alice in Wonderland* in which it was cited one had to run pretty hard just to stay in the same place. But these jobs—will they, you inquire, be devoted to ennobling activities: to fostering wholesome human development, beautifying the environment, caring for the natural world, promoting virtue? Well, no, you're told, that sort of thing tends to be a drain on the economy, because those things are performed in the public sector. The jobs will produce goods and services for the marketplace—products like computer games, and guided missiles, and mobile homes, and services to financial speculators, and leisure industries, and ... I see.

Curious: Tens of thousands of nuclear weapons for national security; economic logic used to make social decisions; knowledge based on a science which ignores courage and virture—the M-1 mind-set brought great benefit in the past but now creates problems faster than it solves them.

Economic production is taken to be the primary basis for the individual's relating to society. The overwhelming proportion of recognized social roles involve having a job in the production economy, being married to someone who has a job, or training to get a job. With modern means of industrial production, many of these roles have ceased to be meaningful and satisfying. Furthermore, as planetary limits to further material growth are approached, and as economic rationality pushes for further automation and robotization of production, the number of jobs will fall increasingly short of the number who want them. Does the society at this point ask itself what meaningful and constructive activities can now be engaged in because economic production does not require the full efforts of all? No, it engages instead in frenzied activities to *increase consumption!*

How does this society make its important decisions?   you ask. The choices that will affect the lives of future generations, of people all around the globe? Through *economic analysis* is the answer. Individual leaders may bring in personal values in arriving at their initial decisions, but the bureaucratic way is to defend decisions with cost-benefit or similar economic analysis. And how does the well-being of future generations enter into such decision making? Economists *discount the future* at a rate of ten percent or more, so the consequences for future generations don't really enter into present decisions. (Many years ago, before the ethic changed, there once was a tradition that the farmer should leave the land for the next generation *better* than he found it. Such sentimental notions fly in the face of "sound" financial management, which puts the emphasis on next quarter's bottom line.)

You ask further into the kinds of decisions evoked by this prevailing economic rationality. It appears that, regrettable as it may seem, society in the United States can no longer afford really good education for every child. It can no longer afford to protect citizens in the city streets at night. It can not even afford to give all citizens the health care they need. On the other hand, extravagant packaging and advertising, wasteful consumption, unnecessary transportation all *add* to the GNP. (Take, for example, the energy required for food production—energy for fertilizer, tractor fuel, long-distance hauling, packaging, freezing, thawing, cooking and so forth. In the end there is many times as much fossil fuel energy as solar energy represented in the food on one's table. That is a situation which may be "economically sound", but surely in the long term is ecologically foolish.)

The dwellers in this society are proud of its being a society of "abundance". Yet you can't help noticing that this abundance and affluence have brought about new forms of *scarcity*—scarcity of natural resources, of fresh air and water, of arable land, of the waste-absorbing capacities of the natural environment, of resilience of the planet's life-support systems, of spirit-renewing wilderness. These are partly a consequence of the forms of technology employed (such as, fossil fuel burning in preference to solar energy sources; non-biodegradable materials; hazardous chemicals; agricultural practices employing vast quantities of artificial fertilizers and pesticides). The "new scarcities" are of course also related to population growth, which in turn is a consequence of improved sanitation and public health measures.

You note another peculiarity: Here is a society whose knowledge system (science) is based on positivism and reductionism. Thus it is a society whose predominant knowledge system ignores altruism, courage, virtue, eternal values, which earns its paramount position through its success in enabling manipulation of the physical environment. In fact, this society boasts of its ability to "control nature"—which seems to you as an alien visitor to be the ultimate in confused thinking since *you* thought human beings were an intrinsic part of "nature".

It is not necessary to go on. Time was when the most serious problems of humankind had to do with satisfying basic needs and dealing with the hazards of the natural environment. The most serious problems of modern society arise from the *successes* of the industrial society paradigm. The horrors of modern warfare, worldwide environmental spoliation, interference with life-supporting ecological systems, progressive resource depletion, widespread poverty and hunger, prevalence of hazardous substances, stress-related disease, the possibility of detrimental climate changes stemming from carbon dioxide buildup in the atmosphere, all are interconnected components of what we might call the one world macroproblem. They are consequences of a mind-set and the behaviors and institutions associated with it—the industrial-society paradigm, with its M-1 metaphysical base—which brought great benefits in the past but now creates problems faster than it solves them. The world macroproblem will be satisfactorily resolved only through fundamental change of that mind-set.

Origins of the World Macroproblem

There is no need here to describe the world macroproblem in detail. Let us briefly summarize the interrelationships among three of its chief aspects: widespread poverty and hunger, environmental degradation, and the nuclear weapons dilemma.

The nuclear weapons dilemma is that there are now, and there will be in the foreseeable future, enough long-range missiles with nuclear warheads, at various places in the world and aimed at various "enemies", to imperil human civilization if not human existence on the planet. At the moment the vast majority of these are in the USA and the USSR. However, the arms race between these two countries is only the present form of the crisis. Who is the enemy or ally of whom is a circumstance which has undergone many changes over the past three-quarters of a century.

Besides, among the countries that now have or will soon have access to nuclear and biological weapons there are some for whom the present world order offers little hope. For most of the vast majority of the Earth's population the goal of becoming a rich high-consumption society (which seems to be the best model the industrialized world has to offer) is forever beyond their reach—for reasons of planetary resource and environmental constraints, among others. Even if the birth rates drop far more dramatically than now seems possible, the Earth's population will continue to increase for decades, and the rich industrialized world—a shrinking fraction of the whole—will be viewed with increasing envy and hostility by the rest.

The world lacks a vision of a viable global future. The industrialized world, having lost any consensus on ultimate meanings and values, steers itself mainly by economic and financial signals serving as pseudo-values. Part of the developing world is scrambling to catch up with the West; other parts are seeking some attractive alternative to scrapping their own cultural roots and adopting the alien culture of the West. Many of the Third World countries are caught up in a global arms race to which there appears to be no end; some are spending more on technically sophisticated arms than on health, education, and social services combined. And some stagger under debt loads such that oppressive interest payments impair their ability to improve their lot.

The global environmental condition worsens steadily, notwithstanding temporary or localized reversals of the general trend of deterioration. Much of this is associated with the economic activities of the industrialized countries—acid rain, toxic chemical concentrations, diminishing and deteriorating water supplies, local environmental degradation. But much of it also is a consequence of the desperate quest of the poor for food, firewood, grazing land, and shelter; it has often been said that poverty is the planet's greatest polluter.

Throughout the world, economic, social, and international policy is being implicitly based on some image of the global future—some picture of how human advancement will take place in diverse societies, as well as how we will husband or exploit the Earth's resources and life-support systems. Practically all of that policy is founded on concepts of global development that seem inexorably to lead toward continuing widespread misery and conflict—because of the gross disparities between the rich and the poor; because of forces pushing peasants off the land and into urban slums; because of the wrenching apart of societies by the temptations and imperatives of modernization; because of deforestation and water pollution and soil destruction and desertification and a hundred other kinds of environmental spoliation; because of sudden wealth stemming from natural resources that are coveted by the industrialized world; because of irreversible changes in plant and animal species, soil composition, and climate. If these trends do not change, continuing conflicts seem inevitable. In a nuclear age they can be perilous indeed.

This macroproblem has its origins in basic assumptions, starting with the M-1 metaphysic. Since there is no "reality" to inner experience, transcendent values have no power and materialistic values prevail. Thus it seems reasonable for society to be characterized by economic rationalization of an ever-increasing fraction of social behavior and organization. Industrialization of production of goods and services gradually extends to more and more of human activities; increasingly, they all become included in the economy. One result is monetization and commercialization (all things coming to be measurable by and purchasable in units of currency). The economic rationalization of knowledge leads to the "knowledge industry": to science justified by the technology it produces; to education justified by the jobs it prepares for. Economic rationality becomes predominant in social and political decision making, even when the decisions it leads to are unwise by other standards (such as the well-being of future generations). Technological solutions are attempted for problems that are basically socio-political in nature. The worth of persons is assessed by their value in the economy. Man's relationship to the Earth is essentially an exploitative one.

From such reasoning and values the components of the macroproblem spring, as is quite apparent to our imagined visiting anthropologist. This is not a totally new or recent observation. The inevitable consequence of trying to run a society from an M-1 metaphysic was apparent to some scholars long ago. One of them was the distinguished Harvard sociologist Pitirim Sorokin.

Sorokin had examined the rise and fall of civilizations in his four-volume work *Social and Cultural Dynamics*, written between the two world wars, which he later summarized in *The Crisis of Our Age* (1941). His conclusion, based on an impressive study of cultural and social indicators for as far back as he could find any records, was that Western society, like some before it, has gone so far in the dominance of "sensate" values that it must almost inevitably swing back, probably to a better balance of inner-directed and outer-directed values. This, however, involves change at the deeper level of basic beliefs—or, to use the in-vogue term, change in the dominant paradigm.

Sorokin described the signs of an impending "transformation", which he probably did not expect quite as soon as it seems to be arriving.

The British historian Arnold Toynbee also anticipated an early end to the industrial era as we have known it. In *A Study of History*, written in the 1930s and 1940s, he made an even more exhaustive study of the evolution and devolution of civilizations. He has been widely interpreted as being pessimistic about the future of industrial society. However, he also spoke of the possible "transfiguration" of modern society into some kind of respiritualized form.

Lewis Mumford was perhaps the most unquenchably optimistic of the lot. Thirty years ago, in a little book called *The Transformations of Man* (1956), he described the previous transformations of Western civilization, fewer than a half dozen. He then went on to outline a coming transformation, the signs of which were invisible to all but a very few:

> Every [human] transformation . . . has rested on a new metaphysical and ideological base; or rather, upon deeper stirrings and intuitions whose rationalized expression takes the form of a new picture of the cosmos and the nature of man. . . . We stand on the brink of [such] a new age: the age of an open world and of a self capable of playing its part in that larger sphere. An age of renewal, when work and leisure and learning and love will unite to produce a fresh form for every stage of life, and a higher trajectory for life as a whole. . . . In carrying [human] . . . self-transformation to this further stage, world culture may bring about a fresh release of spiritual energy that will unveil new potentialities, no more visible in the human self today than radium was in the physical world a century ago, though always present. . . . Who can set bounds to man's emergence or to his power of surpassing his provisional achievements? So far we have found no limits to the imagination, nor yet to the sources on which it may draw. Every goal [humanity] . . . reaches provides a new starting point, and the sum of all [humanity's] . . . days is just a beginning.

More contemporary arguments arriving at similar conclusions can be found in a number of recent books. Alvin Toffler's

The Third Wave (1980) summarizes: "Despite what today's parties and candidates may preach, the infighting among them amounts to little more than a dispute over who will squeeze the most advantage from what remains of the declining industrial system. . . . While short-range political skirmishes exhaust our energy and attention, a far more profound battle is already taking place beneath the surface. On one side are the partisans of the industrial past; on the other, growing millions who recognize that the most urgent problems of the world—food, energy, arms control, population, poverty, resources, ecology, climate, the problems of the aged, the breakdown of urban community, the need for productive, rewarding work—can no longer be resolved within the framework of the industrial order."

The subtitle of Theodore Roszak's *Person-Planet* (1977) summarizes a similar argument: "The Creative Disintegration of Industrial Society" (and the creation of the new). Similar discussions will be found in Fritjof Capra's *The Turning Point* (1983) and Marilyn Ferguson's *The Aquarian Conspiracy* (1980). These various essays emphasize different aspects of a common theme, namely, the necessary transformation of industrial society over the next few decades (a tremendous speedup over any such revolutionary change in the past, largely because of modern travel and communication binding the world into a more tightly interconnected whole).

Clues from Social Movements

What are the salient characteristics of this new post-modern age? We can obtain some clues from seeing what people seem to be asking for, as they interrupt the smooth course of their lives to devote energy to an assortment of social movements.

In the decade of the 1960s a host of social movements came into being or took new form from older movements. There was a peace movement, related to but not the same as the peace movements of the 1920s and 1930s; there was a women's movement, which extended the women's suffrage movement into claims of other rights beyond the vote; an environmental movement growing out of the old conservation movements; a civil rights movement which was in a way an extension of the earlier abolitionist, populist, and labor movements; and so on. One heard a good deal about "radicalization"; certain demonstrations and other activities were carried on, not so much to win a tactical objective as to bring about a "radicalization" of minds, a lessening of the hold of the accepted belief system of the culture.

This radicalization or change of perception was primarily in two forms. One involved altering one's perceptions with regard to what were claimed to be oppressive, regimenting, depersonalizing, alienating, stupefying, stultifying characteristics of modern social institutions. Confrontations with authorities were deliberately set up, for instance, to invoke the "mind-changing" quality of such confrontation. The other form of radicalization was that associated with the sudden interest in yoga, meditation, Eastern philosophical-religious systems, transpersonal psychologies, psychedelic chemicals, and the like. This involved changing self-perception, specifically in recognizing one's essential spiritual nature.

By the mid-1980s this had all changed somewhat. The ecological movement, peace movement, and women's movement are now more clearly recognized to be different drops in a single wave of transformative change. While there is some student involvement, the issues have come to have appeal for many more mature citizens as well. The word "radicalization" is seldom used, and "changing consciousness" has taken its place. This change in consciousness is partly toward perceiving how the whole pattern, the underlying paradigm, of Western industrial society leads inexorably to the kinds of problems and global dilemmas we now face, and toward realizing that the dilemmas have their satisfactory resolution only through change in the dominant paradigm. It is partly toward recognizing that we unwittingly "buy into" belief systems (in which the Earth exists to be exploited, "premodern" cultures are to be superseded, people with non-white skins are inferior, women have a subordinate role, nuclear weapons bring "security", profligate consumption is "good for the economy", and so on); and that a major step is taken when realization comes that the things our society takes for granted are not necessarily true—that it is not necessary to

"buy into" the beliefs. It is partly toward the empowering realization that all institutions in society, no matter how powerful,
obtain their legitimacy from the perceptions of people—and
hence that people have the power to change institutions by
challenging the legitimacy of prevailing institutional behaviors. In particular, the most recent component of this consciousness change is toward recognition that people have the power
to challenge the legitimacy and glorification of war as an instrument of policy for any nation.

Thus, aided no doubt by awareness that the world is steadily
working less well, a contagion of reperception has been spreading around the world for at least the past twenty years, infecting
first the educated middle class but then moving on to exclude
no age, race, or socioeconomic class. Evidences abound in the
forms of survey data, social movements, Green political parties,
book sales, workshops and seminars, and numerous other social indicators. The fraction of the total US adult population involved in a radical reperception is probably no more than
around 5 to 10 percent, most of whom have made the shift
within the last decade. Some of the surveys show as high as 50
percent espousing values that are significantly different than
the values during the high economic growth of the 1950s and
early 1960s. Similar changes are evident in northern Europe,
Canada, Australia, and to a lesser extent elsewhere in the industrialized world, including the Eastern European countries. A
complementary reperception can be found among a smaller "alternative development" group in the Third World.

To characterize this reperception we may identify five aspects: search for wholeness, search for community and relationship, search for identity, search for meaning, and sense of
empowerment.

Search for wholeness. The world had become fragmented,
as had the individual. A technological ethic of "man controlling nature" had contributed to the separation of humans from
the matrix of life around them. With the rise of capitalism the
economy had become separate from, and dominant over, the
rest of society. The steady deterioration of the environment
and violence to natural ecological systems was one consequence. A sense of alienation was another. One's work had be-

come a job, and the job was separate from the rest of life. Religion too tended to be something separate, based on different premises than seemed to prevail in the most powerful of society's institutions.

In a variety of ways—an ecological movement, a holistic health movement, emphasis on quality of work life, an appropriate technology movement—the perception is presently being expressed that life is whole and that there is something wrong with a society that breaks it into fragments.

Having been educated to be specialists and to view the complex whole in "manageable" segments, we are now faced with a multifaceted global crisis which will not be resolved by some technological or managerial "fix". Rather, it is claimed, the resolution will come out of some whole-system view. Just as at the individual level a holistic view of health involves the whole person—body, mind, and spirit—so at the planetary level the problem will prove to be solvable only through a holistic approach.

A key aspect of this wholeness is awareness of the finiteness and multiple-interconnectedness of the planetary ecosystem, the inextricable interdependence of all human communities and dependence on the planetary life-support system. An outlook that has come to be termed "deep ecology" goes beyond the contemporary scientific framework to a subtle awareness of the oneness of all life, the interdependence of its multifold manifestations, and the irrepressibility of its tendencies toward evolution and transformation.

Search for community and relationship. Both urbanization and modern economic realities—most jobs away from home and neighborhood—had brought about a loss of community. Bigness and concentration of power had been among the chief contributors to the feelings of alienation and depersonalization in modern society. A response is taking the form of a rise in the informal economy; intentional communities; an assortment of human relations workshops, group therapies, and other endeavors to relate more deeply with fellow human beings; re-ruralization, decentralization, crafts, and appropriate technology movements. By the latter is meant technology that is human-scale and ecologically compatible, and in general "kind" to human beings and the planet. It includes technologies that enhance rather than diminish the human being; "soft-path" renewable-resource energy technologies and practices; regenerative organic agriculture, with practices of replenishing the soil and natural pest control; holistic health care emphasizing prevention and wholesome relationship to one's own body.

There is also a developing sense of a global community and an appreciation of the richness of the planet's cultural diversity. The tendency of the world industrial economy to obliterate competing cultures is felt to require correction; a global ecology of cultures is the more desirable state, rather than a world covered by Western industrial monoculture.

Search for identity.   In reaction to the depersonalizing aspects of modern society there has been in the industrialized societies a widespread seeking for personal identity, often through psychotherapies and weekend workshops, but often simply in an individual Wanderjahr.   An aberration of this tendency manifested as the "Me Generation" phenomenon of the 1970s.

Beginning around the 1960s, various groups began to resist the homogenization to which modern society is prone, with its mass markets and mass media. Some of these are ethnic groups asserting their differences—the Quebecois, the Basques, the Chicanos.   Others are different in other ways, but asserting their right to be themselves and not feel or be treated as inferior—the handicapped, the aged, homosexuals.

The two largest of such groups are women and the Third World. The women's movement had its early emphasis on liberation and equal rights.   In its more recent form, however, it emphasizes sensitivity to the destructive aspects of patriarchal society and masculine competitive, aggressive, exploitative values—seeking a balance of these with feminine nurturing, cherishing, cooperative, conserving values and appreciation of the feminine perspective.

The Third World groups are struggling to release themselves from their self-perception as inferior, a consequence of generations of Western domination and colonization.   While recognizing the material and managerial accomplishments of Western societies, they are affirming or reaffirming the values of their own cultural heritage.   Thus whereas for a generation after World War II "development" had been assumed to mean economic development in the mold of the Western industrial powers, since the 1970s there has been a quest for "alternative development" more compatible with the peoples' own cultural roots.

Search for meaning. This aspect of the reperception saw Western industrial society in a crisis of meaning and values. No need is so compelling as the need we all feel for our lives to make sense, to have meaning. We will tolerate almost any degree of austerity or risk in this indomitable quest for meaning; we may even choose suicide if we fail. After the "great debunking" of religion by reductionistic, positivistic science, and with the discovery that economic production consumption and even technological achievement are unfulfilling, modern society felt a vacuum in the area of basic values and central meaning.

The incompleteness of positivistic science and its inability to deal with the whole of human experience was challenged by a rapidly developing interest in Eastern philosophical and religious outlooks, and a vast array of explorations of the world of inner experience—from yoga and meditative disciplines to confrontation therapies and psychedelic drug experiences. Within science a similar opening up of interests occurred, manifesting in humanistic and transpersonal psychology, exploration of altered states of consciousness, etc.

There are today multifold signs of a respiritualization of Western society, with emphasis on self-realization, transcendent meaning, and inner growth leading to wisdom and compassion. The picture is complicated because one of the most visible phenomena is the growth of Christian evangelical-fundamentalists—a group who appear to have little in common with the followers of some of the Asian gurus passing through. It is only by talking in depth with many of these people that one discovers underneath a quiet but spreading commitment to an M-3 kind of metaphysical perception.

Sense of empowerment. One of the most striking changes in the past two decades has been the extent to which people are awakening and feeling empowered to take responsibility for their own lives and for changing society as necessary. This has happened in both industrialized and developing countries.

There have been numerous technological issues (particularly since the "technology assessment" movement around 1969) where the people clearly asserted that because of potential consequences around the globe, and effects on generations to come, the issues were too important to be left to the experts. Examples were the SST and ABM, nuclear power, biotechnology. When the people in the US were sufficiently aroused, they effectively halted the Vietnam war. As noted, increasing numbers of people around the world are raising questions about the legitimacy of national policies that imply war as a feasible option.

We just observed that the two "majority groups", women and the Third World, are awakening to the sense of their real, potential power. No economic, political, or military power can compare with the power of a change of mind—in particular, a challenge or withdrawal of legitimacy.

Value Emphases of the Trans-modern World

Assuming for the moment that the main thesis of this book is correct, namely that at the present time we are somewhere in the middle of a shift in prevailing metaphysical assumptions from M-1 to M-3, what does that imply about trans-modern (or trans-industrial) society? Probably at least the following five value emphases are implied:
- Man in harmony with nature
- Man in harmony with man
- Individual self-realization
- Decentralization and an ecology of cultures
- Globalization of global issues

Man in harmony with nature. (We mean the word "man" in the sense of man/woman, or human beings; although if truth be told the disharmony is in good measure due to the activities of the male of the species.) In the M-3 perception of reality we are one with nature, and in harmony with the life processes. Any disharmony is a consequence of faulty perception, and correctable.

This basic harmony contrasts sharply with the exploitative attitude toward nature that has been a hallmark of industrial society. So-called primitive societies typically have had more cooperative, less exploitative relationships with nature. In some cases (for example, many American Indian tribes) there has always been a clear tradition of caring for the Earth. Thus there is much precedent for the ecological ethic that now seems dictated by increasingly serious environmental problems.

The shift toward being more in harmony with nature is coming about only partly through the threat of what will happen to us if we don't change. It is more fundamentally a simple corollary of the M-3 assumptions.

Man in harmony with man. If we are all connected, and in some sense all one, then any disharmony I may feel in human relationships is also a matter of my own perception. The emerging vision emphasizes community in the small view, and global cooperation in the large. Institutions will be more person-centered, and nondiscriminatory with regard to sex, race, and culture.

One of the most important shaping forces is the rebalancing of masculine and feminine influences. The most powerful of the forces shaping the modern world—reductionist science and manipulative technology, competitive enterprise, the aggressive nation-state—were strongly biased toward masculine and patriarchal perspectives. Implicit in the M-3 assumptions is an emphasis on wholeness, involving a creative balance between masculine and feminine qualities—between aggressiveness and nurturing, competition and cooperation, rationality and intuition. Riane Eisler, in *The Chalice and the Blade* (1987), speaks of the change as being from a "dominator" model of society (which has predominated in the West for around 5000 years) to a "partnership" model.

On the world scale there has to be a "great leveling" of rich and poor societies—not in wealth alone, but in equity and equality of opportunity. The Western concept of economic development toward a "consumer society" will give way in favor of "liberatory development" emphasizing liberation of spirit and energy, self-reliance, preservation of cultural diversity and identity, and reassertion of group history. There will be a progressive casting off of the mental yoke of fatalism, self-denigration, and submission to external authority—and increasing emphasis on human productiveness, autonomy, and global cooperation. For these conditions to be possible in the individual societies, there has to be a reshaping of the international order in a manner compatible with the legitimate goals of developed and developing countries.

Individual self-realization. The new order is to be one that fosters movement from self-subordination (to superiors in a hierarchy, to institutions, to "advanced" or powerful nations) toward self-realization. Especially in the workplace and in the development of Third World countries is this emphasis on self-actualization of central importance.

The basic idea involved here is summarized in psychologist Abraham Maslow's concept of "deficiency needs" and "self-actualization" or "being" needs. It appears that persons whose "deficiency" needs (for food, shelter, warmth, sex, belongingness, esteem) are reasonably well satisfied are then motivated by "being" needs. This was well expressed in a counterculture slogan of the late 1960s: "We don't want to have more—we want to *be* more".

Manifestations of this emphasis in the industrialized countries are to be found especially in the various "liberation" movements (of women, minorities, the elderly) and intentional communities, and in the worker self-government and "industrial democracy" movements of northern Europe. In the Third World the emphasis is seen most clearly as an insistence on rejecting the traditional acceptance of poverty and exploitation (by landlords, rich ruling classes, imperialists). In both cases the emphasis is on awakening to the realization that one has been imprisoned by "buying into" a set of beliefs which, once this is realized, one need not accept.

Decentralization and an ecology of cultures. There is implicit in the new vision a repudiation of the centralist tendencies of both capitalist and socialist management and production, as well as of the continued urbanization tendencies of both industrialized and developing societies. Espoused instead is decentralization—of population concentration, of community, of agriculture, of management and control, of technology, of economic production, of mass culture.

The issue of decentralization is particularly apparent in the "appropriate technology" movement with its emphasis on human-scale technology under human control.

The value of cultural diversity will be deeply appreciated. Somewhat as an ecological community has resilience that a single-species community lacks, so the world population is more resilient when it comprises an ecology of cultures whose diversity is a source of enrichment to all.

Globalization of global issues. Coexisting with the decentralization characteristic, and not in conflict with it, is the global management of those affairs which, by their very nature, are concerns of the entire population of the Earth. These include use and care of the oceans and atmosphere, sharing and tempered consumption of nonrenewable and some renewable resources, control of weapons of mass destruction, and control of diffusion of hazardous chemicals.

Symbol of a New Relationship with the Earth

One of the critical arenas in which change is both imperative and ongoing is that of attitudes toward the planet Earth. Since it is obvious that modern man's abuse of the Earth is related to the prevailing image of our relationship to the planet, it is interesting to examine a recently announced scientific concept of the Earth as being in important respects alive. This is the "Gaia hypothesis" which, it must be admitted, has thus far created more impact on the conference circuit than in the halls of science.

James E. Lovelock, a British biologist and atmospheric chemist, is largely responsible for the modern form of the idea that we human beings are not just living motes on a vast mineral ball, but that *the Earth itself is a living organism.* The core notion is that the Earth regulates itself very much like the human body or other living organisms. Somehow, temperature, oxygen levels and other aspects of the composition of the atmosphere and the oceans, soil acidity, and other key environmental conditions are kept within the narrow tolerances necessary to sustain life. Those regulatory processes involve, in turn, the biota—the sum of all living things including plants, animals, and microorganisms. The Earth thus exhibits the behavior (except for a reproductive ability) of a single organism—of a living creature. Lovelock's name for that organism is *Gaia*, the name the ancient Greeks gave to their Earth goddess.

Could a planet, almost all of it rock and that mostly incandescent or molten, really be alive? Lovelock suggests comparison with a giant redwood tree: It is alive, yet 99 percent of it is dead wood. Like the Earth it has only a skin of living tissue spread thinly at the surface.

If the Earth is a living organism, does it also exhibit *consciousness*? That is a question not to be answered quickly, but, as implied above, not to be dismissed either.

Lovelock was hired as a consultant in the early 1960s by the National Aeronautics and Space Administration to help determine if there is life on Mars. While others were busy designing landing craft to go see, Lovelock took a different approach. He reasoned that in the absence of life, the gases in the atmosphere should react in such a way that the whole reaches a state of equilibrium. The presence of life on Earth disturbs this equilibrium, because the Earth's plants, animals, and bacteria are continually injecting gases and energy into the air. As is well known, for example, plants give off oxygen and use up carbon dioxide while animals do the reverse; thus the Earth's atmosphere contains far more oxygen and far less carbon dioxide than it would if the Earth were not covered with its particular life forms. (Mars, on the other hand, gives no such indication of life.)

The amount of oxygen in the atmosphere near the Earth's surface remains virtually constant at around 21 percent by volume, "just right" for the life forms that have evolved. The life forms themselves appear to regulate the amount of oxygen so that it stays "just right". If the proportion should drop even a few percent, many organisms would die; however, the excess of plant life that would result would tend to raise the oxygen content again. On the other hand, if somehow the oxygen content were to rise to 25 percent, fires would burn out of control. That would no doubt reduce the plant life and hence the rate of replenishment of oxygen, so the proportion would tend to go down.

The temperature, too, is apparently regulated by the biota to just what they need. The Earth's average surface temperature has remained between 10 degrees and 20 degrees Centigrade, even through the Ice Ages, and the biota seem to have had something to do with this. Lovelock explains how, using a computer-based model called "Daisyworld". Imagine, for simplicity, a world in which the only life forms are white daisies. Within the temperature range of 10 to 20 degrees, the higher the temperature, the more daisies. But since more daisies means more of the world's surface is covered with white flowers, more sunlight is reflected, causing the temperature to lower. Thus an equilibrium temperature is approached. Adding other life forms into the model (such as rabbits to eat the daisies, and foxes to control the rabbit population) results in a similar phenomenon. Daisyworld exhibits a temperature-regulating behavior (homeostasis) similar to the temperature regulation of the human body.

As another example, the humid tropical forests of the Earth alter the climate in the immediate vicinity, both in terms of temperature and rainfall. Like Daisyworld, they create the local climate they require in order to flourish. But they also remove carbon dioxide from the atmosphere. As they are cut down, that contributes to the rising carbon dioxide level in the atmosphere (which is also increasing due to massive burning of fossil fuels). Through the "greenhouse effect", the blanket of carbon dioxide is causing worldwide temperatures to rise. Thus the fate of the tropical forests affects climate on a global basis.

The *connectedness* of our decisions and our actions to the whole Earth is one key message of the Gaia hypothesis. But another, equally important one is the role of cooperation of all organisms in the evolutionary process.

For example, take the matter of dimethyl sulphide. This chemical is manufactured in tremendous quantities by phytoplankton, microscopic marine algae. It is useful to them because it reduces the harmful effects of drying when they are left on the beach by the ebbing tide. But it also plays an important part in returning sulphur from the oceans back to the land, and a key role in cloud formation over the open seas—part of the "planetary refrigeration system". It seems that another chemical also manufactured by algae, methyl iodide, is part of a similar process for recycling the essential element iodine.

Now, do these and countless other ways in which various parts of the total Earth system are necessary to each other imply some sort of consciousness guiding the evolution of life on Earth? In a science dominated by the M-1 assumptions the answer is simply that the question is absurd.

That extension of the Gaia idea is, on the other hand, implicit in the traditions of American Indians. For example, Black Elk quotes the following prayer of the Oglala Sioux: "O Mother Earth, You are the earthly source of all existence. The fruits which You bear are the source of life for the Earth peoples. You are always watching over Your fruits as does a mother. May the steps which we take in life upon You be sacred and not weak."

Some of the modern exponents of the Gaia hypothesis tend to speak of collective humanity as the "nervous system" of the biosphere, the organ through which it becomes conscious. Presumably this is because of the special properties of the human brain.

Yet clearly the sense in which the ancients and the American Indians experienced the consciousness of Gaia is something else again. That consciousness was presumably present before there were either humans or any other of what we think of as living forms.

To be sure, there is no scientific basis for postulating such an Earth consciousness. On the other hand, it is inherent in the way in which science developed that if the Earth did, in fact, possess consciousness, it is quite likely that science would have overlooked it.

A restricted form of the Gaia hypothesis, including the organism-like self-regulatory behavior of the Earth, seems almost certainly to have made its way into respectable science. Even in that form, it strongly suggests that humans had better pay heed to the extent to which their activities impair or impinge on the regulatory processes.

As to the Earth's being an organism with consciousness, the jury is still out as far as mainstream science is concerned. Yet this concept, with its profound ethical and ecological implications, does not seem all that strange in the M-3 worldview.

The Greeks Had a Word for It.

Where do all these indicators point? Are there any examples of societies which have been based in an M-3 sort of metaphysical perspective?

There's one, at least, of special interest—ancient Greece. Lewis Mumford had pointed to the Greek concept of *paideia* as the nearest thing to a model of the society to come. Robert Hutchins, in *The Learning Society* (1968), had chosen the same ideal—a society in which learning, fulfillment, and becoming human are the primary goals and "all its institutions [are] directed to this end. This is what the Athenians did. . . . They made their society one designed to bring all its members to the fullest development of their highest powers. . . . Education was not a segregated activity, conducted for certain hours, in certain places, at a certain time of life. It was the aim of the society. . . . The Athenian was educated by the culture, by *Paideia*." *Paideia* was the educating matrix of the society; its highest and central theme, according to its foremost scholar Werner Jaeger, was the individual's "search for the Divine Center".

We do not live in the time of the ancient Greeks, and we will not simply repeat their pattern. Our post-modern society may have cybernetic machines instead of slaves, and it may very likely have a deliberate concern with shaping the future that would have been alien to the Greek culture. It may borrow elements from other cultures as well, such as the relationship to the Earth from the North American Indians. But in one central feature it is likely to emulate the Greeks: That is the idea that self-development and the promotion of lifelong learning is the "central project" of a society that does not have to expend a large fraction of its effort simply supplying the necessities of life.

The New Business of Business

These indications of shifts in values, attitudes, and perceptions have an impact on all sectors of society. One of these, the business sector, deserves our special attention.

If there is anything at all to the proposition that a fundamental transformation is already underway, we should see signs in the business community. For one thing, business is all-pervasive in modern society and reflects any major change in any portion of it. Moreover, business makes it its business to be sensitive to changes in its environment, and to respond to them promptly. The modern business corporation is probably the most adaptive institution humankind has ever devised.

One such sign is the growing acceptability in business of the terms intuition and creativity, and the implications thereof. Philip Goldberg, in *The Intuitive Edge* (1983), defines intuition as "a process of knowing without the intervention of reason or analysis". The idea of arriving at insight without a recognizable thought process flies in the face of the ideal of "rational man". (In fact, until recently, it was usually spoken of as "feminine intuition".) Only in the last decade have business journals such as *Fortune* or *Harvard Business Review* begun to publish articles referring to the use of hunches and intuition in business decision making. Management development courses in recent years have been increasingly overt about using such techniques as affirmation and inner imagery to remove barriers to creativity and intuition.

Studies of high-performing people in many fields show that successful, effective people tend to visualize the results they want in their lives and work, and to affirm to themselves that they will accomplish these goals. They create a clear and conscious intention to achieve certain outcomes and then allow that frequently affirmed intention to guide their actions. Rather than planning what they will do and how they will go about it, they start by creating an intensely alive mental representation of the end state. That representation then works through the individual's intuition and unconscious mental processes as he or she makes the multitude of everyday decisions that bring the goal ever nearer.

Charles Kiefer and Peter Senge, in a chapter in *Transforming Work* (1984), note the appearance of a new type of management based on new assumptions about the nature of human beings and complex social systems. People are viewed as fundamentally good, honest, and purposeful, and wanting to make a constructive contribution in the world. The locus of the desire to contribute is internal, not external; it arises from the person's consciousness of his or her relationship to the whole rather than from a desire for the approbation of others. In this view, the fundamental shortcoming of traditional management is its failure to design social systems in which these characteristics of the individual can develop. The new-style managers tend to appreciate the futility of trying to control complex systems from the top down. They focus instead on arranging conditions which foster the individuals' actualizing their own latent creativity, and on evolving highly autonomous business units in which local initiative and control can operate to the fullest extent possible.

The organizations employing this new management style are characterized by:

- A strong and deep sense of purposefulness and a vision of the future
- A high degree of alignment of members at all levels involving commitment to the shared vision
- A shared sense of ownership and personal responsibility for performance
- Decentralized and flexible organizational structures
- An environment that emphasizes growth and empowerment of the individual as the key to corporate success.

The great leaders of the past have tended to be either autocratic or charismatic; the new management style is empowering. Perry Pascarella, executive editor of *Industry Week*, writes in *The New Achievers* (1984):

A quiet revolution is taking place . . . in the business corporation. . . . Although we have been hearing more and more about corporate efforts in human resource development in recent years, we may miss the essential truth about what is happening: Individuals are awakening to the possibility of personal growth and finding opportunities to attain it. The team building we hear about is secondary to the development of the individual. . . . Management is heading toward a new state of mind—a new perception of its own role and that of the organization. It is slowly moving from seeking power to empowering others, from controlling people to enabling them to be creative. . . . As managers make a fundamental shift in values . . . the corporation [undergoes] a radical reorientation to a greater worldview.

The organization that aspires to be excellent, and to gather to itself and retain excellent people, is finding in this new climate that it must seek to create an internal environment that fosters development of persons. Such organizations typically have a strong sense of corporate vision that has been communally developed, and a strong alignment around that vision.

Leaders in world business are the first true planetary citizens. They have worldwide capability and responsibility; their domains transcend national boundaries. Their decisions affect not just economies, but societies; not just the direct concerns of business, but world problems of poverty, environment, and security. Up to now there has been no adequate guiding ethic. Although these executives and their organizations comprise a worldwide economic network, binding the planet together in a common fate, there has been within that network no tradition of and no institutionalization of a philosophy capable of wisely guiding its shaping force.

As we see in this and the succeeding chapter, such a new ethos for business may be in the process of forming. Interestingly, it appears to be forming around an M-3 kind of assumption about reality.

The economic activities of the world business system have been a contributing element in the world macroproblem. But by the same token, world business will be a key actor in the ultimate resolution of the macroproblem. It crosses national boundaries with much more ease than do political institutions, and the business corporation is a far more flexible and adaptive organization than the bureaucratic structures of governments and international public-sector institutions.

In the next chapter we will explore four additional aspects of the macroproblem: the problem of chronic unemployment and underemployment; the problems of global development (including poverty, hunger, and environmental deterioration);

the area of values and politics; and the perplexing problem of seeking national and international security in a nuclear age. These four examinations will make more specific the general assertion made earlier, that when the underlying assumptions change, everything changes. Perhaps not just by accident, everything seems to be changing in a hopeful direction.

6

*Novus ordo seclorum: a new
order of the ages is born.*
                    —Vergil

Aspects
of the
World System Change

It is crucial to understand that a shift at such a fundamental level of belief as we have been considering implies basic change in economic, corporate, financial, political, research, educational, health-care institutions—in all the most powerful institutions of society. As the pressure for these changes becomes more and more evident, it is likely to be accompanied by a good deal of fear. Fear and anxiety are the root cause of the social disruption and widespread misery that have most often accompanied such revolutionary changes in the past. The greater the level of understanding about what is happening, the less anxiety will be present.

To better understand how fundamental a change is involved, let us look a little more deeply into three specific areas where this change is taking place. These are the areas of work, development, and national security.

The Necessity for Redefining Work

There may be no aspect of the future about which people are typically more confused than the role of work in the life of the individual and in society. The reason in part is that we have failed to recognize the full implications of the social and economic changes that have been taking place.

Our present conceptions about work were formed in an era when the primary societal function of work was the production of necessary or desired goods and services, and in which one could foresee no end to the social desirability of increasing the economic productivity of the individual laborer through technological advance. Yet today these assumptions lead to a fundamental dilemma. On the one hand, if labor productivity in a country does not continually increase, the industry of that country tends to become noncompetitive in the international market. On the other hand, if productivity does increase, the economic product must increase (by definition) to maintain the same number of jobs. As various resource, environmental, political, and social constraints tend to limit economic growth, chronic unemployment becomes an intrinsic characteristic of the future. Since that is an unpleasant thought to contemplate, countries and individuals have tended to use tortuous logic and subtly evasive actions to avoid confronting it.

This problem of "superfluous people"—those marginal human beings not fortunate enough to be employed—grows more serious as society becomes more highly industrialized (or "post-industrialized"). Recognition of this chronic nature of unemployment goes back at least as far as 1930, when British economist John Maynard Keynes warned in his *Essays in Persuasion*:

> If the economic problem [the struggle for subsistence] is solved, mankind will be deprived of its traditional purpose. . . . Thus for the first time since his creation man will be faced with his real, his permanent problem—how to use his freedom from pressing economic cares. . . . There is no country and no people, I think, who can look forward to the age of leisure and abundance without a dread. . . . It is a fearful problem for the ordinary person, with no special talents

to occupy himself, especially if he no longer has roots to the soil or in custom or in the beloved conventions of a traditional society.

Because understanding the changing role of work is so important, let us take the time to look fairly deeply into the history of work in the United States. While the story would be somewhat different in another country, what has happened in the United States has been influential in other industrial countries.

History of work in the US. The fundamental social doctrine of eighteenth-century colonial America strongly emphasized the dignity of labor. It stressed the virtue of diligent application to one's task and promised that earnest industry would be unfailing in its rewards. The values of diligence, sobriety, and thrift, characteristic of the rising middle class in England, were transported to America and became a dominant influence in the colonies. Accomplishment tended to be measured in material progress—the transformation of nature and development of useful arts and knowledge.

Personal aggrandizement was considered more or less incidental, and there were injunctions against waste, extravagance, and ostentation. Labor was scarce, returns from the individual's work were high, and opportunities to move to higher status were abundant. It was assumed that the idle poor brought poverty upon themselves; poverty was made so disgraceful that a man would labor to the extent of his capacity to avoid such a stigma. If not everybody prospered, the great majority of honest, hard-working men made their own way and improved their lot. Additional rewards of the virtue of work were found in the good opinion of others and the sense of having fulfilled one's "calling".

By the nineteenth century, a greater emphasis on self-improvement had developed. The self-made man, less moved by piety and virtue, still owed his advancement to the cultivation of God-given talents and habits of industry, sobriety, moderation, self-discipline, and avoidance of debt. Aiming to surpass the previous generation and provide for the next, he deferred gratification and lived for the future, patiently saving and accumulating. Wealth became more of an end in itself;

compulsive industry, discipline, and self-denial were the means to that end.   The public schools, available to all, inculcated industrial discipline, self-reliance, orderly habits, punctuality, workmanship, versatility, and obedience.   They offered vocational training and served for industrial recruitment, selection, and certification.

The early twentieth century evidenced more stress on the will to win.   The advent of mass production had brought an ever-growing hierarchy of supervisors and managers, and increasingly large staffs for engineering, management, distribution, and sales.   Ambitious young men had to compete with their peers for the attention and approval of their superiors in order to advance in the corporate structure.   Advancement was assumed to depend on willpower, self-confidence, energy, and initiative.   The new ethos was one of salesmanship, boosterism, pursuit of wealth, and success as an end in itself.   There was no apparent reason to question the role of work in either the individual's life or in society.   It was self-evident that the individual worked to support himself and his family.   As for society, the assumption that the role of work is industrial production, shared by economists from Adam Smith to Karl Marx, was widely accepted.

The great Depression of the 1930s signaled the end of labor scarcity and the beginning of a persistent fear of job shortages and chronic unemployment.   That anxiety was put aside during World War II, but resurfaced as the war drew near to an end, and worries were expressed about the coming unemployment situation "when peace breaks out".

Part of the supposed solution to this problem was found in a Keynesian reasoning based on several new principles:

1. Mass consumption is necessary to enable all members of a society to enjoy a high material standard of living; mass consumption is also necessary to support mass production in an industrial economy.
2. Mass consumption cannot exist or continue unless there is a mass distribution of purchasing power.
3. Full employment is necessary to create this mass distribution of purchasing power, and bring about prosperity and

well-being for all.

4. It is an appropriate function of government to promote full employment through promoting mass consumption and economic growth, and to insure that any who are left out of this participation in the mainline economy are adequately taken care of with social security measures.

Thus around 1950 the United States became a mass-consumption society—"throwaway society" it was termed then. People learned to consume and waste; to "use it and throw it away". They learned that frugality was no longer a prime virtue; rather, it was bad for the economy. Consuming became the new ethic; people began to call one another "consumers". They learned about "planned obsolescence"; about needing to replace things with new models, either because the old ones fell apart or because the new model was more fashionable.

Another boost to the economy came from the Cold War and the global arms race. Particularly during the period just after World War I, Americans generally considered sales of arms to other nations to be highly unethical and immoral. By the late 1950s ethics had given way to practicality, and US sales representatives, in and out of uniform, were urging nations around the world that they needed more high-technology US-produced weapons.

From 1946 on there were several attempts to legislate full employment into existence. The social costs of unemployment were recognized as being very high. To be unemployed in modern industrial society is to suffer a severe blow to one's self-esteem. Much evidence links employment to psychological health, and unemployment to emotional disorders, alcoholism, disease, drug use, and crime. If it were possible to create ample, satisfactory work opportunities for all, many of the social problems would disappear. But despite the heroic pronouncements of the "Great Society" era of the 1960s, the unemployment threat steadily worsened.

Current concepts of the coming "Information Society" are in part a reaction to that veiled threat. What do you do when the productiveness of the economy has risen to where the needs of society can be met employing only a fraction of the potential work force? Answer: Become obsessed with consumption, to try to use up the product and keep the machinery running. What do you do when technology has advanced to where anything you can train a human to do, you can train a computer (robot) to do; and furthermore the computer will probably do it better, faster, and cheaper? Answer: Become obsessed with economic growth to create new jobs for humans to do. And what will create that consumption, and that growth? Answer: *Information!* We can all develop an insatiable appetite for information, to be passed around at an exponentially increasing rate. Demand for information-related services can be made to increase at such a rate that we need not fear the further job-displacement effects of the computers. Never mind that mindless consumption of information services in order to create jobs may not be the choice of thinking people, any more than was boundless consumption of food as a response to increasing agricultural productivity. (Perhaps instead of Information Society we should call it "Makework Society".)

Chronic unemployment and underemployment. There is reluctant but growing admission in the United States (and in Northern Europe) that despite mass consumption and global arms races (and despite the advent of the "Information Society"), the long-term future of industrial society is characterized by chronic unemployment and underemployment (working at less than one's full productive capacity). The reasons are basically two: (1) in the long run, economic growth may not continue to generate enough jobs to accommodate the expanding work force; and (2) the quality of available jobs may not be compatible with the rising educational levels of the work force.

The problematic character of economic growth arises primarily from the tension between growth and the cluster of problems associated with resources and the environment. These problems could be eased if economic growth were modified to lessen resource utilization, since the economy displays a built-in correlation between economic product and resource utilization. But a slacking of growth increases unemployment. Thus despite a commitment to growth and full employment, environmental constraints and resource limitations will tend to keep the economy from generating enough satisfactory jobs to meet the demand.

Economic and demographic trends are partially obscuring this problem through the 1980s, especially in the United States. Earlier in the decade the labor force in the US was increasing at a rate of something like two million persons per year (2 percent growth rate). Both the postwar baby boom effect and the effect of the rapid entry of women into the labor force have been dropping off, so there is a temporary reduction in labor force growth rate. Thus there is a temporary easing of the national unemployment problem, but the long-term prospects are another story.

Despite the fact that the unemployment/underemployment dilemma seems intrinsic to the industrial paradigm, economists and social scientists are divided on how fundamental the problem will appear in the future. This lack of agreement probably reflects, in part, different perceptions of the extent to which the problem already exists. One gains perspective by imagining what would happen to unemployment rates in the US if by some miraculous means sustained global peace were to become a reality and the portion of economic activity now involved with national security were no longer needed. Already we can hear the panic reactions whenever there is talk of canceling a defense contract or space project or shutting down an airbase. The true extent of the unemployment problem is further reflected in inflated age and education criteria for job entry, delays imposed on job elimination or automation of routine operations, subtle forms of featherbedding, and pressures on older employees to retire early.

Underemployment too is a major source of alienation and workplace problems. As the educational level of the work force rises, discontent and alienation spread among highly educated workers forced to take jobs previously performed by workers with less schooling. Education is no longer a sure route to increased status, power, and income. Neither does it insure work that is intrinsically challenging and that offers opportunities for creativity and self-expression.

Persons of high educational achievement tend to expect that their work should utilize their talents and develop their poten-

144 Global Mind Change

tial. But disappointment awaits many of those who anticipate managerial, technical, and professional positions, with middle-class income and status to match, which include opportunities for growth, challenge, and self-fulfillment. Increasing numbers of well-educated workers must accept jobs—white-collar as well as blue-collar—that are routine, stultifying, and unchallenging. A significant fraction of the jobs in industrialized society are neither intrinsically challenging nor obviously related to inspiring social challenges.

The nature of underemployment is revealed by the ancient story of two stonecutters who were engaged in similar activity. Asked what they were doing, one answered, "I'm squaring up this block of stone." The other replied, "I'm building a cathedral." The first may have been underemployed; the second was not. Clearly what counts is not so much what work a person does, but what he perceives he is doing it for.

The frontiersman, the old-time craftsman, the farmer blessed with a fine piece of land, all would have scoffed at the idea that they were underemployed. But once mechanized agriculture appeared on the scene, one could no longer spend the day behind a horse and plow in the same spirit as before. Once a robotized assembly line can mass-produce an item, the challenge to make the same item by hand is destroyed.

"Meaningful work" is not necessarily work that is exciting and challenging every moment; it may, rather, be work that is part of a larger endeavor which is infused with meaning. If the society has a "central project" in which people believe—for example, conquering a geographical or technological frontier, or building a new society or a new world democratic order—then even routine tasks take on meaning.

Unemployment in different perspective. Let us now look at all of this with fresh eyes. There is no doubt that, by and large, the history of industrial society has been a fantastic success story. In only a few centuries Western Europe leapt from the relatively low capability and motivation to manipulate the physical environment that characterized traditional society to a technological capability so high that almost anything one can imagine wanting to do seems achievable. The "wave" of industrial society spread around the planet, affecting in time practically every society on the globe—seducing with its glitter those it did not take over by force.

During those centuries a central focus on economic production seemed to make sense. Providing new tools, making persons' labor count for more, converting more and more of the Earth's resources into economic products, exercising increasing "control" over the natural environment through technology, drawing more and more of people's activities into the monetized economy (both as jobs and as "consumed" services)—all appeared to result in a raised material standard of living, and hence to increased human well-being.

But then we get to the hypothetical situation Keynes identified. What if a society advances technologically until it looks as though economic production of all the goods and services the society can imagine needing or desiring (or all that the resources and environment can stand) can be done with ease, using only a small fraction of the population?

The main answer so far appears to be to continue attempts to create jobs by stimulating economic growth. There won't be enough jobs, so those left out can be taken care of by transfer payments. In effect, the old ethic of "work in order to eat" seems to be changing to "the fortunate may work; the remainder will be kept as pets—supported, with little more demanded of them than that they be housebroken". One needs only to look at the northwestern part of England to get an advance glimpse of what this society will be like.

Another approach is talked about here and there—to treat work as a scarce commodity to be rationed. That concept is at the heart of various extant proposals and programs embodying work-sharing plans, limitations on the work week, and so forth. (This approach doesn't seem terribly sensible, when you think of all the room for creative work in the world.)

But both of the above approaches overlook how basic this shift really is. Contemporary theories of business and labor, of employment and welfare theory, of liberal and Marxist analysis, are all based on the assumption of production-focused society. *What if this central assumption is really obsolete?*

Let us be more specific. It once may have made sense in production-focused society to think of an ever-increasing fraction of human activities being treated as commodities in the mainline economy; to assume the desirability of mainline-economy jobs for everyone; to have thinking dominated by concepts of scarcity, secrecy, and money exchange. With the new era this may all prove to be obsolete reasoning.

For example, informal and underground economies are serving many people today who can't make it into the mainstream. Cooperative sharing fits some situations better than money exchange. "Information society" is not going to solve the problems; the current unenforceability of copyright and patent laws shows the fallacy of considering information to behave like other "commodities" such as tomatoes and automobiles. Furthermore, we are clearly experiencing a breakdown of the leadership and government forms which are based on the assumption that information will be available only to the few.

If one views the situation again from the vantage point of an anthropologist from outer space, one sees clearly that an entirely new mode of thinking needs to be adopted, wherein the widespread elimination of human work which machines can be trained to do is taken as a stimulus to rethink and reexamine the basic assumptions of production-focused society. Society needs to take on a new "central project" now that keeping economic production in that position no longer makes sense. The assumption that income distribution should be linked strongly to jobs in the mainline economy needs to be reassessed.

Society's new "central project". The required new thinking, compatible with emergent value emphases, can be simply stated: In a technologically advanced society where production of sufficient goods and services can be handled with ease, *employment exists primarily for self-development, and is only secondarily concerned with the production of goods and services.* This concept of work represents a profound shift in our perceptions with implications that reverberate throughout the entire structure of industrial society. It is hard to imagine it prevailing in a society dominated by an M-1 metaphysic and confused about meanings and values. If the whole society shifts to an M-3 perspective, the picture is a much more promising one.

We referred earlier to the Greek concept of *paideia*. In the Greek "learning society" the primary function of society, and of all its institutions, was assumed to be to promote learning in the broadest possible definition. *Paideia* was education looked upon as a lifelong transformation of the human personality, in which every aspect of life plays a part. It did not limit itself to the conscious learning processes, or to inducting the young into the social heritage of the community. *Paideia* meant the task of making life itself an art form, with the *person* the work of art. In theory, at least, the achievement of the human whole—and of the wholly human—took precedence over every specialized activity or narrower purpose.

The motivations and values implicit in the M-3 assumptions fit very well with this Greek concept of a "learning society". They clearly do not fit with mindless consumption, material acquisition, and endless economic growth.

In the "learning society" the occupational focus of most people is learning and developing in the broadest sense. This focus includes a wide diversity of activities such as formal education, research, exploration, self-discovery, various specialized roles, and participation in the community of concerned citizens to choose a better future. These activities contribute to human betterment and fulfillment. They are humane, nonpolluting, and nonstultifying. They can absorb unlimited numbers of persons not required for other sorts of work.

"Learning society" implies reversal of a number of aspects of the long-term industrialization trend. It almost certainly involves something like the "intermediate technology" or "appropriate technology" concepts of E. F. Schumacher and others. These terms refer to technology that is resource conserving, environmentally benign, frugal in the use of energy, relatively labor intensive, and understandable and usable at the individual or community level. Such technology tends to complement a strong ecological ethic; strong identification with nature, fellow human beings, and future generations; a lifestyle characterized by voluntary frugality ("doing more with less"); appreciation of the simple life and simple virtues; and the kind of work that fosters these attitudes.

It is premature to try to speculate in more detail what are some of the specific changes that this shift in thinking entails. As we saw in the last chapter, this basic concept is already being discussed in contemporary management; a number of small innovative corporations can be found that are deeply committed to the principle. What it eventually implies for the overall economy is less clear, but the change will not be a small one.

Redefining Global Development

Among the forces shaping the future, surely one of the most potent and long-range is the awakening of the "sleeping giant" usually referred to as the "developing world". The developing world comprises approximately three-quarters of the world's population (about half of them living in China and India), and the fraction is projected to increase to around four-fifths by the end of the century. Most of the countries that make up the developing world were, prior to World War II, either colonies of, or strongly dominated by, the industrialized powers. But those who have for so long accepted the role of privation, inferiority, and servility are less and less willing to do so.

For the two decades following World War II, development was more or less taken to be synonymous with economic development—that is, with "modernization" and industrialization. In other words, the prevailing assumption—in developed and developing countries alike—was that it is the destiny of all peoples on the Earth to follow the path of the United States and the other industrialized countries (with perhaps some differentiation along the capitalism-socialism dimension). That is to say, they would assimilate Western culture (with some small remnant of the original culture left, of course, to encourage tourism and promote products of native crafts).

We have earlier noted that people who spend their lives in different cultures literally experience different realities. Those who grow up in industrialized societies perceive reality in a very different way from an Australian aborigine or a Bedouin or a Hopi. A Native American once characterized the Amerindian outlook as: "(a) everything in the universe is alive; and (b) we are all relatives". Such a perception would be totally foreign to most educated Americans or Europeans. Similarly, the typical American would find it difficult to realize that the implicit goal in US society of ever-increasing consumption of goods and services might be viewed by an outsider as totally insane, or that the assumption that the "natural resources" of the Earth exist to be exploited is madness.

Thus the implicit objective of modernization has been rejection of the reality of the traditional culture and substitution of a foreign perception. However, the realities of some of the traditional cultures are proving to be more resilient than expected. Increasingly, cultural leaders in the developing countries have come to see that optimal development of people in the broadest sense is not necessarily fostered by abandoning their own cultural roots and adopting the alien culture of Western industrial society. Thus there has been growing insistence on a different international economic order and on exploring development paths other than "modernization".

In a speech the day before his death, E. F. Schumacher, author of *Small Is Beautiful* (1974), said of development aid that it is "a process where you collect money from the poor people in the rich countries, to give it to the rich people in the poor countries." Development, he said, could not center around bringing the technologies of the highly industrialized countries to the developing countries. "This kind of industry has no future. Nature cannot stand it, the resource endowment of the world cannot stand it, and the human being cannot stand it."

If these attitudes continue to strengthen, as seems likely, the thrust of global development will not continue to be, as at present, toward Western industrial monoculture around the globe. Rather, it will be toward an ecology of diverse cultures, each with its own interpretation of human development, societal goals, and ultimate meaning—and toward a world system that tends to support rather than diminish, thwart, and bias against this diversity. The momentum and influence of the single industrial world economy is so great, however, that any such change in the development thrust is tantamount to major change in the world's economic and financial institutions.

The potential impact of world attitude shifts on the future of the world economy is often ignored. For example, since the world economy runs on energy, dwindling fossil fuel reserves is a matter of concern: World public attitudes will be decisive as to whether augmenting and eventually replacing fossil fuels by some form of nuclear power leads to an acceptable future, or whether some form of "soft energy path" must be found instead.

World public opinion will be similarly critical with regard to how drastic measures will be demanded for dealing with serious environmental deterioration, and with increasing problems of hazardous substances, toxic wastes, and agrichemical runoff. Pressures of economic competition would seem to dictate rapid deployment of robots and artificial intelligence in industrial production and service industries; the spectre of rising world unemployment may spawn opposing reactions. Spreading public perception that negative long-term consequences of the activities of large corporations may outweigh benefits has already implied a significant challenge to the legitimacy of present corporate behaviors.

How powerful these changes in world attitude may eventually become is difficult to foretell. In a series of documents from the International Labour Organization and other United Nations agencies relating to Third World demands for a "New International Economic Order", a set of universally felt human needs has been defined as being in essence:

- Basic human needs ("enough" food, shelter, health care, education, employment, and security of the person)
- A sense of the dignity of being human
- A sense of becoming (a chance to achieve a better life)
- A sense of justice or equity
- A sense of achievement, of being involved with something worth achieving
- A sense of solidarity—of belonging to a worthy group and of participating in decisions that affect the group's, and one's own, destiny.

National-level programs aimed at implementing the concept of a right to satisfaction of these universal needs have been adopted by over 120 countries, in most cases within the past three decades. In some of the countries, including the United States, the programs were preceded by many years of debate over the appropriateness of this presumed right and its actualization through provision of "safety-net" transfer payments or provision of services. Yet inequities in economic distribution far beyond anything that would be tolerated in any individual country exist between the rich and the poor internationally. Behind the rhetoric of the demands of the developing world for a new economic order is the proposition that *a concept of human welfare which has thus far been accepted and applied within a majority of individual nations should now be extended to the entire family of humankind.*

Despite inevitable opposition, ultimate acceptance of this proposition appears likely, in that it is an extension of an already accepted basic trend, and that the various peoples of the world are increasingly aware of being one world, through communication and commerce (as well as shared fate of the planet).

Perhaps most central of all aspects of the development conundrum (which is intimately linked to the underemployment/unemployment dilemma) is that of *meaning.* Traditional society, whatever its drawbacks, had a place for everyone—a role to play, with its own inherent meaning. Modernization has involved the destruction of traditional meaning and the creation of marginal people—people who live at the margins of society and have no real place, whether unemployed, underemployed, or unemployable. It will not be allowed to continue to do so. The triumphs and horrors of anti-modernization movements in Iran and Cambodia are only early indicators of the irrational forces that will bring about change if more reasoned approaches do not.

To depict the problems of modernization is not to overlook the positive accomplishments of the same paradigm that contributes to the dilemmas. We are not simply indulging in a criticism of industrial society, rather, we are attempting to indicate one compelling reason that the future will inevitably differ from a continuation of past trends. It is of critical importance to understand what social forces propel us in a different direction—why a fundamental system change is unavoidable.

The development problem and the work problem are intimately related, and alike in one respect. They both arise out of the fundamental issue of modern society—namely, what is it all about? What is the *meaning* in the success of modernization? If the "learning society" is an answer for the technologically advanced countries, the "developing society" is an answer for the world: "developing society" in the sense of fostering the maximum possible development for each human individual.

Surely it is not too idealistic to imagine a future global commonwealth in which each of Earth's citizens has a reasonable chance to create through his or her own efforts a decent life for self and family; in which men and women live in harmony with the Earth and its creatures, cooperating to create and maintain a wholesome environment for all; in which there is an ecology of different cultures, the diversity of which is appreciated and supported; in which war and flagrant violation of human rights in the name of the state has no legitimacy anywhere, and there is universal support of the rule of law throughout the world; in which throughout the entire human family there is a deep and shared sense of meaning in life itself.

If that goal is an inspiring definition of development, it will serve equally as a definition of true *security*.

Finding Global Security

In the foregoing, we have described the signs of shifting basic assumptions underlying American society in particular and Western-dominated society in general. This shift appears to be away from the M-1 assumptions, which for generations up to the 1950s at least, had been steadily increasing in influence, and toward the M-3 assumptions. These assumptions have never had widespread popular approval in either Europe or America, although the undercurrent has always been present (from the Gnostics and mystery religions, to the Rosicrucians and Freemasons of later centuries, to the New England Transcendentalists of the mid-nineteenth century, and the still later Theosophical movement in England and America and the Anthroposophy movement on the Continent).

We have seen how the various interconnected dilemmas of modern society appear to be built in to the basic paradigm of industrial society, and will become solvable only with a shift away from that paradigm to some as-yet-unspecified trans-industrial or post-modern paradigm. We have seen, also, how the M-3 assumptions are compatible with the diverse traditional societies around the globe. Thus one might hope that with a shift toward the M-3 metaphysic the scourge of war might be finally eliminated from the Earth. Let us explore that possibility in more detail.

Removing legitimacy from war. In this nuclear age, practically everyone is for peace. However, not all mean the same thing by the word. Some stress "peace with national security". Others insist that there must be "peace and social justice". Some praise the nuclear weapons for having "kept the peace for 40 years"; others find that being under perpetual threat of nuclear holocaust is a state that hardly qualifies as a definition of peace.

Whatever way the world eventually comes to handle the issue of peace, or more specifically, prevention of nuclear war, that task must be done *with one hundred percent reliability*. Nothing less will do; the world cannot afford *one* nuclear war. It is sobering to realize that nowhere else in our experience is that kind of reliability demanded.

In considering this goal, it will be helpful to distinguish between two kinds of peace: (1) a long-term goal of "real peace", implying permanently low levels of conflict, and prevailing attitudes of loving, caring, and peacefulness among persons and nations around the globe, and (2) a short-term goal of "practical peace", sufficient to remove the threat posed by presently available weapons of mass destruction and mass slaughter (nuclear, biological, chemical). The former goal is, in effect, a major step in social and psychological evolution. We have been urged toward it by spiritual leaders of East and West for thousands of years; yet progress is slow. The latter goal we must achieve now.

By "practical peace" let us mean something even more specific. This goal would include, at a minimum, (a) delegitimation of both war and preparation for war as instruments of national policy; (b) outlawing of all weapons of mass slaughter; and (c) meaningful commitment by all the powerful nations to pool sovereignty to a sufficient extent to create and maintain an effective institution for peacekeeping and nonviolent conflict resolution.

The two goals, the long- and short-term, are of course intertwined. Progress toward one aids achievement of the other. Yet the differentiation is important in a practical sense. Some of the roots of conflict go very deep into the human psyche and some of the perceived injustices involve long-standing characteristics of social and political institutions. Because the long-term goal involves extensive changes in powerful and deep-rooted social and politico-economic institutions, and major transformations in the lives of hundreds of millions of people, it is easy to be overwhelmed by the magnitude of the task. One may be so intimidated that one may overlook the achievability of the short-term goal, which could be realized within a reasonably short time, in a generation or less.

Although it has become fashionable in the United States to malign the United Nations, the Charter of this organization (1945) and the Universal Declaration of Human Rights (1948) must rank among the most noble political documents in history. They have been agreed to by practically all of the nations and peoples of the Earth. They provide one—perhaps not the only—framework within which the goal of "practical peace" could be achieved, if we really wanted it. The plain fact is that the people and leaders of the most powerful nations have not manifested the will to delegitimate war. It is not a matter of lack of appropriate mechanisms, or of need for new technologies, but a moral choice.

We should not overlook the progressive delegitimizing of certain forms of war that has been quietly taking place. Until around 1914, *offensive* war was considered permissible and legitimate, at least under certain conditions. Some of the European nations rather frequently fought wars that were frankly offensive in purpose. By the end of World War II wars of aggression and territorial gain were generally considered to be not permissible, and since about mid-century most military engagements around the world have been justified on defensive grounds. (In 1947 the United States changed the name of its War Department to the "Department of Defense".) The "gunboat diplomacy" in which powerful, technically advanced nations intervened at will in weak Third World nations, although it may still go on to some extent, must be well disguised if it is to be considered legitimate even by the people of the nation committing the intervention.

Attitudes toward war have been changing rapidly as the fundamental nature of war changed. Since World War II, war is no longer a contest between trained armies; it is the desolation of civilian populations. In World War I approximately 15 percent of the casualties were civilian; in World War II, over 50 percent; in the Vietnam war, close to 90 percent. One can only imagine what the figure would be for a nuclear war. Serving one's country in war, which as recently as World War I was regarded as "glorious" and "heroic", has so lost its glamor that the veterans of Vietnam complain about being treated like pariahs. It is difficult to be enthusiastic about being a participant in the mass slaughter of innocent victims.

We have before us the example of progressive withdrawal of legitimacy from various forms of slavery, oppression, torture, and murder that were formerly condoned or even encouraged. Delegitimating war and preparation for war, seeking national and global security through other means, is the next logical step in the sequence.

Throughout history, the really fundamental changes in societies have come about not from dictates of governments and the results of battles but through vast numbers of people changing their minds—sometimes only a little bit. Some of these changes have amounted to profound transformations—for instance the transition from the Roman empire to medieval Europe, or from the Middle Ages to modern times. Others have been more specific, such as the constitution of democratic governments in England and America, or the termination of slavery as an accepted institution. In the latter cases, it is largely a matter of people recalling that no matter how powerful the economic or political or even military institution, it persists because it has legitimacy, and that legitimacy comes from the perceptions of people. People give legitimacy, and they can take it away. *A challenge to legitimacy is probably the most powerful force for change to be found in history.*

The nineteenth-century Prussian strategist Karl von Clausewitz defined war as "an extension of state policy by other means". To move from this rational argument for war to a complete delegitimating of war would be one of the more profound shifts in the history of humankind. Yet like other major shifts in attitude throughout history (for example the end of feudalism, the delegitimating of political colonies), it can come about when the people of the world change their minds and demand it. The only kind of war which retains the cloak of legitimacy is that for which the preparation was in the name of "defense", and the initiation is non-deliberate. *That is precisely the kind of war that is most hazardous—the one which the world fearfully awaits.*

Beliefs and perceptions in international conflict. The main obstacle to the removal of legitimacy from all war is *lack of belief in the feasibility of peace.* We have alluded earlier to the extent to which our perceptions, motivations, values, and behaviors are shaped by partially unconscious beliefs such as "It is fundamentally a world of scarcity", or "People with other-colored skins are alien". Scientific research has been progressively disclosing the surprising extent to which this "inner map" of beliefs underlies perceptions, which in turn underlie conflict and the perceived impossibility of peace.

If it is these inner beliefs that are really at the core of intergroup conflicts, the nature of the task of achieving peace becomes more clear. It is not human nature that has to change—as has sometimes been claimed—but, rather, the unconscious "programming". (Observing this, some scientists have actually urged interventions such as implanted electrodes with reconditioning signals to bring about desired "peaceful" behavior. We restrict our discussion here to self-chosen reconditioning.)

We humans have a truly awesome ability to deceive ourselves. Once we have settled on one perception of "reality", all evidence to the contrary tends to become invisible, all hints that our picture might be wrong or even seriously incomplete are deftly (and unconsciously) warded off. This is true even if the perception doesn't serve our self interest. For example, the paranoid sees the environment in a way that causes much self anguish, and rational argument or even contradictory experience may fail to change that perception. It does not serve us well to perceive the world in such a way that there is no viable alternative to the nuclear weapons impasse, yet that is the all too common perception. In fact it appears that *a vast number of persons would risk the destruction of civilization rather than risk fundamentally changing their perceptions of the world.*

Consider the implications if we were to be persuaded that *the fundamental causes of non-peace on the planet are to be found mainly in the collective beliefs of the various societies— beliefs which are partly consciously held, but are in great measure unconscious.* We are used to seeking explanations of the state of global non-peace in national competitions, in the ambitions and frustrations of leaders in those countries, in the flaws of past treaties, in conflicts between religious and ideological factions. No doubt these explanations are partially accurate. But underlying them, as a more fundamental breeding ground of non-peace, are the largely collective beliefs that so subtly create barriers, separations, tensions, and collisions. These beliefs are difficult to even become aware of, and certainly to challenge, mainly because the people around us in our own society tend to share the same beliefs and tacitly to take them for granted.

Naturally enough we all have our own internal resistance to perceiving how the underlying paradigm of Western industrial society (both forms: capitalist and Marxian) leads inexorably to the kinds of problems and global dilemmas we now face. We have earlier described how we unwittingly "buy into" a belief system in which technical solutions are sought for problems that are basically sociopolitical in nature—including the futile attempt to buy "national security" through more powerful weapons. We are most reluctant to recognize how powerfully the world's belief systems, including our own, lock us into a death march toward the future.

Collectively held unconscious beliefs shape the world's institutions, and are at the root of institutionalized oppression and inequity. "Peace" will always be no more than a temporary truce if there exist widespread perceptions of basic injustice, needs unmet, and wrongs unrighted.

To the empowering principle that the people can withhold legitimacy, and thus change the world, we now add another: *By deliberately changing the internal image of reality, people can change the world.*

We have spoken earlier of the principle (so puzzling to the M-1 assumptions; so matter-of-fact to the M-3) that what we deeply believe and image to be true tends to become real. But what we deeply believe and image to be true can be changed through changing what we persistently affirm to ourselves. A large portion of the Earth's population is using this principle, unwittingly. In myriad ways we see people reaffirming fear, despair, the inevitability of nuclear holocaust, their powerlessness to do anything about it. Think of the power this collective negative affirmation wields in bringing about the very thing we fear and wish to avoid. And think of the power it would have if the world were to deliberately affirm the feasibility of "practical peace" within a generation.

One's initial reaction to the idea of imagining a peaceful world is likely to be that it sounds like a simplistic version of "the power of positive thinking". It may seem difficult at first to convince oneself that by such an affirmation one is actually doing anything. True, it may be simplistic to believe that if we all just love one another and speak peace, peace will come into the world. It may be simplistic because powerful unconscious forces make our love ambivalent, and our peace tinged with hidden conflict.

Despite such justifiable caution, it remains the case that a collective belief in the achievability of global peace will contribute toward realizing that goal, just as the collective disbelief is now thwarting it. However, for affirmation to work well we need to be as specific as possible. The affirmation of sustainable peace will be most effective if it is not simply a general "pray for peace" outlook, but rather affirmation of a fairly specific plausible scenario based on an informed view of the factors and forces involved.

People sincerely busy with some sort of peace activity often fail to recognize the subtleties of the principles involved here. Holding a negative image—dwelling on and even trying to generate the fear that a nuclear exchange might come about, or holding anger toward our leaders who continue to escalate the numbers of missiles (while talking arms limitation)— contributes very directly to bringing about what is feared or hated. *Being against war is not at all the same thing as being for peace.* Holding a positive image, vividly imagining a state of peace to exist, contributes to that state's coming about in ways that may seem quite mysterious if we have too limited a belief about the capabilities of the human mind. Because of the interconnectedness of all minds, affirming a positive vision may be about the most sophisticated action any one of us can take.

Politics and Values

We have implicitly raised the question of what business might be like if it were restructured on the base of an M-3 set of assumptions—and found, perhaps to our surprise, that it already shows signs of moving in that direction. We raised a similar question regarding development, and saw that although in the past development has been equated with modernization and has tended to overrun and drive out transcendental beliefs in traditional cultures, a small "alternative development" movement is seeking new patterns of development—at least some of which implicitly contain something like the M-3 assumptions. If we now look to political systems, we may notice that there is an element of M-3 hidden away in the orientations of the "Greens" parties in various countries.

Green politics a portent? Green politics in West Germany arose out of the feeling that the most fundamental and critical issues of the day were not addressed by the central positions of any of the existing parties. Among the broad spectrum of citizens who rallied during the mid-1970s to stop the spread of nuclear reactors, the pollution of rivers, and the death of the forests, there arose an understanding that we humans are part of nature, not above it; all our complex structure of governmental and economic institutions—indeed human life itself—ultimately depends on wise, respectful interaction with the life-support processes of the planet. As a growing group of people perceived the interconnections among principles of ecological wisdom, sustainable peace, an economy with a future, and a participatory democracy with power channeled directly from the grassroots level, they conceived of Green politics as the political expression of these concerns.

Greens-related parties have played significant political roles in fifteen European countries and another half dozen elsewhere. The Greens parties are sometimes misidentified as being on the left. "Left" is usually associated with tendency toward the welfare state, public ownership of critical industrial and service organizations, and strong emphases on egalitarian and human rights issues. Although Green politics is concerned with human rights and social responsibility, its primary focus is quite different from that of the classical Left. The Left tends to take for granted the goals of technological progress, economic growth, and material standard of living, assuming that increasing wealth will enable resources to be applied to problems of social justice and human rights. Green politics finds a fundamental flaw in this logic, and judges that more fundamental change will be required. As the Greens parties tend to claim, "We are neither right nor left; we are in front".

The Green outlook includes emphasis on a holistic view, ecological awareness, ending the nuclear arms race, decentralization, human-scale technologies and enterprises, feminine perspective, trans-materialist beliefs, social responsibility, nonviolent change, and the empowerment of people. There is a keen sensitivity to the destructive aspects of patriarchal industrial society; specialization and bureaucratization; and masculine competitive, aggressive, exploitative values. What is sought is a balance of these values with a more holistic view, and with the feminine nurturing, cherishing, cooperative, conserving values. There is an emphasis on self-realization, transcendent meaning, and inner growth leading to wisdom and compassion. That there is a dimension of spirituality to Green politics seems unquestionable, yet there is a reluctance to identify the movement as such in so many words. The concept of "deep ecology" is one of the adopted ways of talking about spirituality in terms that are inoffensive to those who, for various reasons, eschew religious language. "Deep ecology" goes beyond the scientific framework to a subtle awareness of the oneness of all life, the interdependence of its manifold manifestations, and the irrepressibility of its tendencies toward evolution and transformation.

M-3 in the founding of the United States. For the most important example of a political system based on M-3 principles, however, we need to look back two centuries to the early shaping of the United States of America. Most Americans seem unaware that a particular embodiment of the "perennial wisdom", in the Freemasonry of the time, was a key factor in the American democratic experiment. The philosophy that underlies Freemasonry has gone by many names since its progenitor appeared in the Egyptian mystery religions. It was a behind-the-scenes influence throughout the development of Western civilization, and in the latter half of the eighteenth century it played a leading role in the emergence of democratic philosophies of government.

Freemasonry as it existed at that time was both esoteric and political (in contrast to contemporary Masonic lodges, which are much more in the nature of social organizations). The essential premise of Freemasonry was that there are transcendental realms of reality in which we coexist, and of which we potentially can have conscious knowledge. While the patterns and forces of these realms are inaccessible to the physical senses, they are available for exploration through looking into the deep mind. They play important roles in shaping evolutionary and human events, and can be called upon for power and guidance.

The Freemasonry network of the eighteenth century transcended national boundaries; there were lodges in Great Britain, France, and Poland as well as America. Freemasonry was concerned with more than the development of individual awareness. Most particularly, its concern focused on the development of human knowledge and the arts, and on the reformation of governments toward a "philosophic commonwealth" and democratic forms.

The most obvious evidence of this influence in the shaping of the United States is in its Great Seal, adopted in essentially its present form in 1782. (Considerable opposition was expressed to the Presidential decision in 1935 to place on the new dollar bill this "dull emblem of a Masonic fraternity", as professor Charles Eliot Norton referred to the central symbol on the reverse side—the unfinished pyramid capped by the "All-seeing Eye".) If one imagines that the founders of this country were a motley citizenry of farmers, shopkeepers, and country gentlemen, the Great Seal symbols from the ancient traditions of Freemasonry seem a puzzling choice. But Benjamin Franklin and George Washington were both active and high-ranking Masons. Of the 56 signers of the Declaration of Independence, at least 50 were Masons; so were all but five of the 55 members of the Constitutional Convention. Many Freemasons from other countries supported the American Revolution, including Lafayette, Kosciusko, de Kalb, and Pulaski. Offshoots of the secret Masonic societies of Europe were transplanted to the New World at least 15 years before the Revolution, with the express purpose of initiating a democratic experiment that had not found fertile soil in Europe.

The Great Seal of the United States with its symbolic references to development of individual awareness, human knowledge and the arts, and to the reformation of governments toward a "philosophic commonwealth".

The symbols of the Great Seal depict a vision that not only sustained and guided the new nation through most of its history, but also for a time provided inspiration to the poor and downtrodden around the world. Bearing in mind that it is the essence of a powerful symbol that it says many things to many levels of the mind (so that any "explanation" of its meaning is necessarily a dilution and distortion), let us examine the symbols of the Great Seal as they appear on the back of any dollar bill.

The most obviously Masonic symbol is the uncompleted pyramid capped by a radiant triangle enclosing the All-seeing Eye, which occupies the center of the reverse side of the seal. Whatever other meanings this ancient symbol may have had (such as significance attached to the numbers of levels and stones; or resemblance to the Great Pyramid of Gizeh, shrine tomb of Hermes who personifies Universal Wisdom), it clearly proclaims that the works of men (either individual character or external works) are incomplete unless they incorporate divine insight. This symbol is meant to indicate that the nation will flourish only as its leaders are guided by supraconscious intuition.

The phrase *novus ordo seclorum* (from Vergil), meaning "A new order of the ages is born", declares that this event is not just the formation of another nation but of a new spiritually based order for the world. The project is launched with confidence because *annuit cœptis*, "He [God] looks with favor upon our undertaking".

Dominating the obverse of the seal is the bird that is now an eagle, but in earlier versions was the Phoenix, the ancient symbol of human aspiration toward universal good, of being reborn through enlightenment and higher awareness. The olive branch and arrows in the bird's talons announce that the new order covets peace but intends to protect itself from those who would destroy it.

E pluribus unum, "unity from many", refers to the nation made up of states; probably also to the higher unity. The star-studded glory over the bird's head traditionally symbolizes the cosmic vision.

The "great debunking" of religion by M-1 based science that took place over roughly a century extending into the 1960s took its toll as regards the values underlying the great American democratic experiment. By the 1970s, the prevailing mood was largely one of obliviousness to the meaning of the symbols and cynicism with regard to the goals. The power of these symbols on the collective psyche is such, however, that if the American nation is to regain its earlier position of moral leadership in the world it will be through an effort focused around these symbols and meanings, and no other.

Leading-edge Change: An Example

We remarked earlier that one might (somewhat paradoxically) anticipate that the world of business, which on the one hand is so totally a product of the Western industrial paradigm, would at the same time be one of the first sectors to adapt to the new—first co-opting some of its slogans, lifestyles, and superficial values, but in the end being transformed by it. The early signs of this are already apparent in the organizational development and executive development fields. It will be fruitful to look at one example.

Larry Wilson is a several-times successful entrepreneur, earlier the founder of Wilson Learning Corporation which purveys courses in sales, administration, management and leadership. He founded and operates the Pecos River Learning Center on a 2000-acre ranch in northeastern New Mexico, which aims at providing advanced training for tomorrow's top executives. Its clients are the no-nonsense managements of large to very large corporations.

Larry is convinced that a new day is dawning for business leadership. Most of those who pass through his workshops are, too. What they are learning is of interest, not only because it points toward new characteristics of the business world, but because it summarizes the key insights of the leading edge of our culture.

The following four "learnings", says Wilson, are the key to successful leadership (and living) in the new era. It will be helpful to think of them as exemplifying the sort of understanding that makes obvious sense from the vantage point of the M-3 assumptions, and would have seemed dubious at best viewed through the M-1 lens.

Fear and trust. Fear and inability to trust are two of the most important limiting factors for executives (and the rest of us). Fear of criticism, of ridicule, of failure keeps us from actualizing our potentialities—to a far greater extent than is immediately apparent. Because we can't trust, we try to do by ourselves what can't be done alone. The most important thing to learn about fear and trust is that both are *choices*—unconscious choices, but choices nonetheless. That is to say, we can *choose* to trust and not to fear.

One of the good ways to learn about fear and trust is experientially. For example, fear can be faced in attempting to scale a cliff or performing some feat in a high place (with a safety harness), so that one is faced with the necessity of dealing with the fear of (seemingly) risking one's life. Trust is learned in a group activity in which the goal can clearly not be reached without depending on one another. (In one such exercise, Wilson has the team go over an eighteen-foot wall without the use of any aiding implements. To do this they have to form a human pyramid to get the first person over—and eventually a human chain to hoist over the last person. The lesson of the necessity for trust and cooperation is learned at a deep experiential level.)

Another effective approach to fear and trust is through affirming something like the following: There is nothing in the universe to fear. I can trust. I can trust my own mind (although the teachings of my culture are that in the unconscious lurk evil and unsavory things, and one must not go exploring without the aid of a psychiatrist). I can trust others (although life seems to present much evidence to the contrary). I can trust the universe to provide for my needs. (We may recall the advice: "Do not be anxious. . . . Consider the lilies in the field, how they grow; they neither toil nor spin; yet . . . even Solomon in all his glory was not arrayed like one of these. . . . Therefore do not be anxious about tomorrow.")

To affirm "I have no fear", or "I trust", is in a sense to lie to myself—just as the athlete is lying to himself when he affirms "I am leaping gracefully over the bar set at 7 feet 10 inches", knowing that he has never jumped that high in his life. But the point is, he is programming himself to do just that. Similarly, in the process of affirming absence of fear and total trust, one is programming the self to perceive the world as different—and to find it different in experience. (Recall in firewalking the temporary suspension of belief that "burning coals barbecue bare feet" results in immunity to harm.)

Purpose. The second learning is that each of us can discover, deep within ourselves, a sense of purpose—of having chosen to come here to do something. To align our lives with that purpose is the closest thing to a "secret of life" that can be given. To structure an organization around the goal of helping each individual find and act from that deep sense of purpose is to assure a limitless source of motivation.

Yet we typically experience great resistance to that inner alignment. We do not have to seek very far for the reason. To have the goal of aligning one's desires with the deep inner purpose implies having *no other goals*. No other aims, ambitions, plans, hopes, ideals, desires, preferences, predilections, formulas of morality, reputation for virtue or consistency or good sense, rational analyses of preferred actions—nothing else. (We will recognize the familar emphasis in the Eastern traditions on nonattachment, or in the Christian tradition on "losing all to find all".) The ego-mind balks, feeling its control threatened.

Again we can use the "reprogramming" power of affirmation and inner imagery. An affirmation such as "I have no other desire than to know the deepest part of myself, and to follow that", vividly imagined to be true, and repeated many times daily over months, will produce changes that are startling.

Creating a vision. The sense of purpose is not specific enough to form a basis for action; it is necessary to create a vision. We do this all the time, without thinking. Often as not the vision does not serve us well—such as the vision "I'm afraid I may fail", or "I am trying hard to achieve" (thus affirming that it is difficult).

Once the vision is created and there is commitment to it, the factors and forces to bring about its realization are already set in motion. "Coincidences", "lucky breaks", and "following hunches" are likely to play a part; actualization of the vision comes about in ways that feel mysteriously like something more than planned steps plus chance events. Exertion is unnecessary—exertion is the inner struggle between conditioning and the deep intuition.

The more vividly and persistently the vision is held, the stronger the tendency for it to actualize. If it is the collective vision of a group or an organization, that is even more powerful. Thus it follows that real leadership is helping the group to create a vision that is as nearly as possible in alignment with their individual sense of purpose, thus assuring the motivation to achieve it without the need of external carrots or sticks. Effective management seeks to foster commitment to a shared vision of the future, and to develop a high degree of alignment around that vision among members at all levels.

The same insight has application in the area of fundamental societal change. The key step in our bringing about change is eschewing the negative visions to which we have unwittingly been contributing, and choosing a vision that befits our inner purpose and that of those around us.

Acting with feedback. The vision is the basis for action, and action is essential. But because none of us can discern clearly just what action will lead to achievement of the goal, whatever action we take is likely to be off target. The essence of the fourth learning is to consider *whatever* happens—success or failure, good luck or bad, opposition or unexpected help—as *feedback*, informing us on the appropriateness of the action.

Thus one is unattached to a specific outcome. It doesn't matter whether the action achieves the goal. It doesn't matter if the action generates opposition, or encounters obstacles, or seems to end in failure. It doesn't even matter if the goal turns out not to be what we really want. Only one thing is essential— the inner decision to follow the deep sense of purpose and to consider all else as feedback from a basically friendly universe.

As this way of life becomes a habit, we look back over our lives and discover much more of a pattern than we were able to discern at the time. Past decisions were somehow made in a way that contributes to our present competence and understanding, even though we were unaware of it at the time. Skills developed along the way, knowledge gained, will all be used in the tasks to which our inner leanings now direct us. Our external lives are much as they were before; enlightenment has not led to the necessity for putting on white robes, gathering followers, and building temples. Life is as it was before—but with a profound difference. It could be characterized as a deep, quiet knowing, and a deep joy. The joy is unaffected by adversity, or apparent failure, or opposition, or criticism—because, again, these are all accepted as feedback signals nudging us toward the path we most deeply desire for ourselves.

Because of the interconnectedness of all minds with the universal mind, we can be sure that the tasks to which we are directed will be most effective in solving the world's fundamental illness, of which hunger and poverty and plague and pestilence and war are all a part. We need not fear that in pursuing our own real self-interest we will fail to contribute maximally to the real self-interest of others.

Concluding Thought

We have concluded with these four "learnings" because it would be difficult to improve on them as a concise summary of the way of life that comes from, or is implied by, betting one's life on an M-3 set of assumptions. Just random informal conversation is enough to demonstrate that the number of those who are so basing their lives is growing rapidly. The crisis in meaning and values that was so evident in the 1960s is quietly being resolved. What once seemed a conflict between science and religion is being healed by one simple observation: There is no conflict between the "perennial wisdom" of the world's spiritual traditions and a science based on M-3 assumptions. The number of scientists who are reconciling their science with the M-3 assumptions is small, but increasing. Leading-edge institutions such as some small entrepreneurial corporations are choosing corporate goals, following personnel practices, and encouraging leadership in accordance with the same assumptions. Those are the signs that suggest the global mind change is well underway.

It is difficult for any of us to fully comprehend what is undoubtedly true: *If* the basic assumptions underlying modern society are indeed shifting in the way we have suggested, it follows that *society will, only a few generations from now, be as different from modern industrial society as that is from society of the Middle Ages.* Furthermore, it will be different in ways that we can only vaguely intuit, just as a Renaissance futurist would have had a hard time trying to describe modern society.

We do have an advantage, over any other time in history. When other profound change took place, those living through it tended to be unaware of the historical significance, and aware mostly of the transition pains and difficulties. We are fortunate enough not only to be able to watch major change take place within a single lifetime, but also to possess enough knowledge to have a good picture of what is going on. Our part in it can be exhilarating and fun. Given the choice, why not perceive it that way?

References and Further Reading

* John Adams (ed.), *Transforming Work*; Miles River Press, 1984.

Henri Bergson, *Creative Evolution*; University Press of America, 1984.

* Morris Berman, *The Reenchantment of the World*; Cornell University Press, 1981.

* David Bohm, *Wholeness and the Implicate Order*; Routledge and Kegan Paul, 1980.

* John Briggs and David Peat, *Looking Glass Universe: The Emerging Science of Wholeness*; Simon and Schuster, 1984.

* Fritjof Capra, *The Turning Point: Science, Society, and the Rising Culture*; Bantam, 1982.

* Alex Comfort, *Reality and Empathy: Physics, Mind, and Science in the 21st Century*; SUNY, 1984.

* Bill Devall and George Sessions, *Deep Ecology: Living as if Nature Mattered*; Peregrine Smith, 1985.

Riane Eisler, *The Chalice and the Blade*; Viking, 1987.

* Marilyn Ferguson, *The Aquarian Conspiracy: Personal and Social Transformation in the 1980s*; J. P. Tarcher, 1980.

Philip Goldberg, *The Intuitive Edge*; J. P. Tarcher, 1983.

* Willis Harman and Howard Rheingold; *Higher Creativity: Liberating the Unconscious for Breakthrough Insights*; J. P. Tarcher, 1984.

* Edward Harrison, *Masks of the Universe*; Macmillan, 1985.

Robert Hutchins, *The Learning Society*; Praeger, 1968.

Aldous Huxley, *The Perennial Philosophy*; Harper Brothers, 1945.

Arthur Koestler, *Beyond Reductionism*; Beacon Press, 1971.

Thomas Kuhn, *The Structure of Scientific Revolutions*, 2nd edition; University of Chicago Press, 1970.

James E. Lovelock, *Gaia: A New Look at Life on Earth*; Oxford University Press, 1979.

James E. Lovelock, "Geophysiology: A New Look at Earth Science". *Bull. Amer. Meteorological Society*, vol. 67, no. 4, April 1986, pp. 392-397.

* Abraham Maslow, *Toward a Psychology of Being*; 2nd edition; Van Nostrand Reinhold, 1968.

* Robert Muller, *New Genesis: Shaping a Global Spirituality*; Doubleday, 1979.

Lewis Mumford, *The Transformations of Man*; Harper Brothers, 1956.

Jacob Needleman, *A Sense of the Cosmos*; E. P. Dutton, 1976.

Perry Pascarella, *The New Achievers*; Free Press, 1984.

* F. David Peat, *Synchronicity: The Bridge Between Matter and Mind*; Bantam, 1987.

* Kenneth Pelletier, *A New Age: Problems and Potentials;* Robert Briggs Associates, 1985.

Michael Polanyi, *Personal Knowledge;* University of Chicago Press, 1958.

Karl R. Popper and John C. Eccles, *The Self and Its Brain;* Springer International, 1981.

Milton Rokeach, *The Open and Closed Mind;* Basic Books, 1960.

Theodore Roszak, *Person-Planet: The Creative Disintegration of Industrial Society;* Anchor/Doubleday, 1978.

E. F. Schumacher, *Small is Beautiful: Economics as if People Mattered;* Abacus, 1974.

Rupert Sheldrake, *A New Science of Life;* Frederick Muller, 1981.

Pitirim Sorokin, *The Crisis of Our Age;* E. P. Dutton, 1941.

Roger Sperry, "Changing Priorities"; *Annual Review of Neuroscience* (1981), vol. 4, pp. 1-15.

Roger Sperry, "Structure and Significance of the Consciousness Revolution"; *Jour. Mind and Behavior,* Winter 1987, vol. 8, no. 1, pp. 37-66.

* Brian Swimme, *The Universe is a Green Dragon;* Bear & Company, Inc., 1984.

* Charles Tart, *Waking Up: Overcoming the Obstacles to Human Potential* (based on the principles of G. I. Gurdjieff); New Science Library/Shambhala, 1986.

Pierre Teihard de Chardin, *The Phenomenon of Man;* Harper Torchbooks, 1961.

* Robert Theobald, *The Rapids of Change: Social Entrepreneurship in Turbulent Times;* Knowledge Systems, Inc., 1987.

Alvin Toffler, *The Third Wave;* William Morrow, 1980.

Arnold Toynbee, *A Study of History* (abridgement by D. C. Somervell); Oxford University Press, 1947.

United Nations, *Charter* (1945) and *Universal Declaration of Human Rights* (1948). Available from United Nations, New York.

* Renée Weber, *Dialogues with Scientists and Sages: The Search for Unity;* Routledge and Kegan Paul, 1986.

Ken Wilber, *Eye to Eye: The Quest for the New Paradigm;* Anchor/Doubleday, 1983.

* Ken Wilber (ed.), *Quantum Questions: Mystical Writings of the World's Great Physicists;* Shambhala, 1984.

---

* NOTE: The books marked with an asterisk (*) are available through the Institute of Noetic Sciences Books and Publications department. (The list is updated yearly and selections are subject to change.) Members of the Institute can purchase the books at a 15% discount, but the books are available to anyone at the usual retail price. Call 415-331-5650 (9 to 5 PST) for further information.

Index

About the Author

Willis Harman is President of the Institute of Noetic Sciences, Sausalito, California. The Institute is a nonprofit research and educational organization founded in 1973. Its purpose is to expand knowledge of the nature and potentials of the mind, and apply that knowledge to the advancement of health and well-being for humankind and the planet.

For 16 years prior to assuming that post, he was a Senior Social Scientist at SRI International of Menlo Park, California. He initiated a program on futures research, exploring the national and global future. In this capacity he worked on long-term strategic planning and policy analysis for an assortment of corporations, government agencies, and international organizations.

Harman is also emeritus professor of Engineering-Economic Systems at Stanford University, and a member of the Board of Regents of the University of California.

Harman received a BS degree in Electrical Engineering from the University of Washington (1939), and an MS in Physics and PhD in Electrical Engineering from Stanford University in 1948. He taught for several years at the University of Florida before joining the Stanford faculty in 1952. He was a Fulbright lecturer on statistical communication theory at the Royal Technical University in Copenhagen during 1959. He was a reserve officer on active duty in the US Navy during World War II.

Through the 1960s Dr. Harman was active in the newly formed Association for Humanistic Psychology, serving as a member of the Executive Board and as a member of the Editorial Board of the *Journal of Humanistic Psychology*. He was a member of the Commerce Technical Advisory Board serving the US Department of Commerce from 1973 to 1977.

Dr. Harman is the author of numerous texts and papers in various aspects of electrical and systems engineering, futures research, social policy and analysis, and the current societal transition. He was listed as an "exemplary futurist" in the World Future Society's reference work *The Study of the Future* (1977). He authored *An Incomplete Guide to the Future* (W. W. Norton, 1979), and was co-author of *Changing Images of Man* (with O. W. Markley, Pergamon, 1982), *Higher Creativity* (with Howard Rheingold, Jeremy Tarcher, 1984), and *Paths to Peace* (with Richard Smoke, Westview Press, 1987).

The Institute of Noetic Sciences

The nonprofit Institute of Noetic Sciences was founded in 1973 by astronaut Edgar Mitchell to expand knowledge of the nature and potentials of the mind and spirit, and apply that knowledge to the advancement of health and well-being for humankind and our planet. Edgar Mitchell chose the word *noetic* from the Greek "nous" meaning mind, intelligence and understanding. For the Institute, the "noetic sciences" are those that encompass diverse ways of knowing: the reasoning processes of the intellect, the perceptions of our physical senses, and the intuitive, spiritual or inner ways of knowing.

The Institute funds scientific research by others and conducts their own research projects; brings top level scientists and scholars together to share their methods, perspectives and knowledge; and serves the general public and their members as a credible source for information about this important research and the people and ideas behind it.

Major programs include:

Inner Mechanisms of the Healing Response

Creating a scientific understanding of the mind/body relationship has been a fundamental goal of the Institute. Currently, they operate a research program devoted to studying the mechanisms of the healing response. For example, what are the innate processes within us that stimulate recovery and natural self-repair? Is there an unknown healing system that promotes remission from normally fatal illnesses? The Inner Mechanisms Program supports proposals from selected researchers and supports targeted interdisciplinary working conferences on mechanisms of healing.

• *Psychoneuroimmunology:* What are the systems of linkage between the brain, mind and immune system? Can these links mediate self-healing in a significant way?

• *Spontaneous Remission:* What is the evidence for the existence of spontaneous remission? Which kinds of diseases are more "remission prone?" Which kinds of people experience remission and why? The Institute has created the largest database in the world of medically reported remissions and has begun to sponsor remission research.

• *Spiritual Healing:* How do prayer, meditation and spiritual beliefs affect healing? Does spirituality mediated healing operate by even more powerful pathways than those involved in remission? What is the psychophysiology of "miraculous" healing?

Exceptional Abilities

The Institute hopes to create a vital contemporary vision of constructive human potential—a vision that incorporates all that is known about the further and higher reaches of human nature. By studying people with outstanding and extraordinary capacities, the Institute hopes to learn more about the ways that individuals can better realize their unique capacities—and, with them, create a world that supports human fulfillment.

Exceptional abilities range from *exceptional mental functioning,* including lightning calculation and extraordinary memory, to *exceptional physical performance,* such as outstanding performance in sports and feats of endurance. They also include *exceptional psychological functioning,* such as creative altruism and exceptional well-being; *giftedness and creativity,* such as child prodigies; *paranormal capacities,* such as remote viewing; and *exceptional states of awareness,* including peak experiences and altered mind/body perception.

The Altruistic Spirit

In the Altruistic Spirit Program, the Institute studies the human capacity for unselfish love and creatively altruistic behavior. They hope to discover the conditions that foster or suppress creative altruism, and encourage its presence in everyday life. The Institute's annual *Temple Awards for Creative Altruism* honor one or more people who exemplify the altruistic spirit—the irrepressible light of love in the heart of humanity.

New Paradigms—In Science and Society

The Institute's New Paradigms Program explores the relationship between consciousness—particularly values and beliefs—

and global issues, and the premise that *a fundamental change of mind* may be occurring worldwide. Program areas include:

• *Expanding the Foundations of Science:* The Institute is attempting to identify and illuminate what they see as the changing *foundations* of science—evident in the exciting new developments in physics, biology, the neurosciences, systems theory and other fields. These developments provide startling insights into understanding the basic processes of health and healing, psychology, parapsychology, sociology and international relations. In fact, the Institute believes these changes in the very foundations of science will generate a "global mind change" every bit as sweeping as the dramatic change in worldview accompanying the scientific revolution in the seventeenth century.

• *Global Peace and Common Security:* In the past the Institute promoted a positive vision of the possibility of world peace through citizen diplomacy projects and publications such as *Global Mind Change, Paths to Peace,* and *The Peace Packet.* The Institute's vision of what makes a peaceful world now includes environmental, economic and human rights issues as well.

• *The Role of Business:* More and more business leaders are realizing their corporate "mission" includes people development, education, and helping solve global problems. The Institute works with an international network of visionary executives and entrepreneurs to explore the role of intuitive leadership in business, advance adult learning and creativity, and employ corporate resources to create a positive global future.

The Institute's pioneering research and educational programs are financed almost completely by donations from members and other sources of private support.

Members receive the Institute's quarterly journal, the *Noetic Sciences Review,* which offers a serious discussion of emerging concepts in consciousness research, the mind/body connection and healing, and our changing global reality; and *Special Reports,* which provide a deeper look into specific issues in these areas. They also receive the quarterly *Noetic Sciences Bulletin,* which offers reports on continuing Institute projects, member activities, and upcoming conferences and lectures; and the triannual *Noetic Sciences Catalog,* a comprehensive resource guide to the many books, audiotapes and videotapes in this field, which are available to Institute members at a discount.

The Institute for Noetic Sciences
475 Gate Five Road, Suite 300
Sausalito, California 94965-0909
(415) 331-5650